I0214710

NEVADA

A Strange State

By Rudi Kraft and Mary Venable

Special thanks go out to my dear wife, Mary Venable.

Without her help this book would have taken much longer to complete.

© 2015 Rudi Kraft and Mary Venable

Published by RK Marketing

All Rights Reserved

ISBN 978-0-9965346-0-4

No part of this book may be reproduced or transmitted in any form or by any means, electronic or mechanical, including photocopying, recording, or by any information storage and retrieval system, without written permission from the publisher.

All drawings by Rudi Kraft.

Printed and bound in the United States of America.

The weird, the funky, the unusual…

Nevada has it.

Aliens and nukes

Showgirls and reclusive millionaires

Miners and eccentrics

Gangsters

Ghost towns

Dragons

…

So turn the page and get ready!

The Dam Builders

They built the dam

their shovels now rest,

They are now gone

their memories fade.

Their lives were hard

hard as the land

they took the chance

they tamed the west.

but they were here

their monument stands.

Rudi Kraft

1873

This Winchester Model 1873 was found leaning against a tree in 2015 in the Nevada desert. Who left it and why is a mystery. A rifle like this was a valuable item at the time, and possibly a life saver.

A Clever Chimp

Washoe, a chimpanzee raised in Reno, was able to communicate with humans through 350 words of American Sign Language she had been taught.

Al Bramlet

Former secretary/treasurer of Culinary Union Local 226 in Las Vegas. Built the union into the powerhouse it is today with a membership of about 35,000. Disappeared after stepping off the plane from a trip to Reno. His body was found in the desert several weeks later, riddled with bullets.

A Real Big Lion

The bronze lion in front of the MGM weighs 50 tons.

Adaven

Is Nevada spelled backwards. Two towns had that name and they both have disappeared. One was between Pioche and Tonopah and the other in Elko County. The last one existed for an amazing five years, from 1911 to 1916.

Adverse

This is what railroad people call a track that runs counter to the grade. The town of Adverse is a siding near McGill along the eastern border of the state. That town has fallen on hard times since the mine closed some years ago.

A Wash

A wash is a waterway that is filled with water only during storms. It is extremely dangerous because of soil conditions and topography in desert areas. You could be standing in bright sunshine without even a hint of rain and have a wall of water coming at you because of rainfall in the mountains miles away. It happens time and time again. The water comes, the water goes. It is mostly all over within hours.

A huge wine cellar

The largest wine cellar in the country can be found at the Rio hotel. Allegedly 65,000 bottles are stored there.

Airstream Park

On Fremont Street in Las Vegas, next to the Container Park. These modern versions of the aerodynamic aluminum travel trailers of the 1930's are a minimalist living experiment with only 200 square feet of living space. There are also micro houses on the site, with 150 square feet of living space. Well worth a visit.

Alamo

In the Pahranagat Valley. This is the place to be for petroglyphs. Hundreds of ancient rock writings.

Alcohol and Nevada Law

As with so many other things, alcoholic beverage laws in Nevada cannot in any way, shape or form be compared to those of other states. Nevada and, specifically, Las Vegas is as wide open as can be. But there are still some minor rules to be observed, silly as they may seem. Las Vegas is essentially divided into two parts, the Strip, and Downtown. The dividing line is Sahara Avenue at the SLS Hotel. North of that hotel is the City of Las Vegas proper; south of it is Clark County. In other words, the Strip is not in Las Vegas at all. Basically you are allowed to booze it up 24 hours a day, seven days a week. There are numerous bars and taverns that are open around the clock. Another thing about Nevada: you are responsible for your own actions. If you stagger out of a bar dead drunk and you get into trouble, it's on you. Your friendly bartender wants to sell booze, he/she is not your babysitter. This all stems from the Old West days, when some towns had more bars than stores. Here are a few simple rules to keep you out of trouble:

No drinking of alcohol within one thousand feet of a church, synagogue, public or private school, hospital, homeless shelter, or withdrawal facility.

Liquor purchased in a closed container may not be consumed on the premises or within one thousand feet of where it was bought.

But, if a drink is purchased in an open container, a plastic cup for example, you can take it and drink it in public.

No glasses or glass bottles on the Strip, but plastic cups all day long.

No open containers on rides. Empty your class before you catch a ride.

Observe those few simple rules and get sloshed to your heart's content. It's Vegas, baby.

Nevada is also the only state to prohibit local and state laws from making drinking a public offense.

Alexander von Humboldt

Was a German nobleman and explorer who spent years traveling in the American West and from there into South America. He made extensive records of every rock, plant, animal and insect he could find. He then traveled down the Orinoco into the Amazon and out to the east coast of Brazil, just to prove it was one river system and not two. Really amazing. His diaries and finds can now be found at the A. v.

Humboldt Institute in Berlin, Germany. I was amazed to see a statue of him in Mexico City one day.

Amargosa

Amargosa has its share of odd things. There is the opera house, the haunted hotel and this, the Area 51 Alien Center.

Alien Cat House

A legal brothel specializing in extraterrestrial experiences. It is off U.S. 95 in Amargosa Valley.

America's Loneliest Highway
Interstate 50

Runs west to east. Nothing but desert and jackrabbits. Hundreds of miles of the same. Once in a while a ranch in the distance. Bad place to break down. Closed once in a while for road racing. European people love this road.

Anthony "The Ant" Spilotro

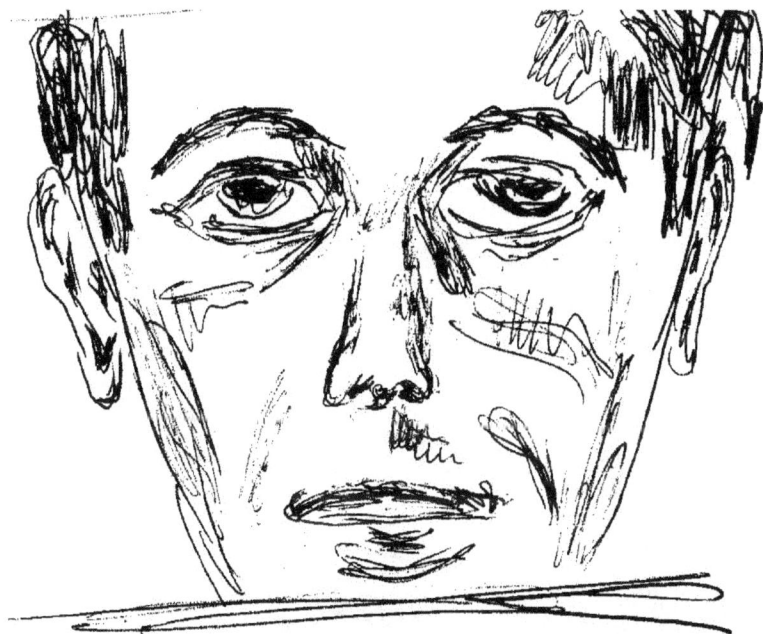

Not a nice man at all. His body is somewhere. He and the "New Hole in the Wall" gang tried to rob a jewelry store once by poking a hole in the wall. Inside were the cops waiting for them. Not too clever. Joe Pesce's character in the movie "Casino" was based on him, if that tells you anything. That movie was thinly veiled real life with the names changed. Robert DeNiro's character was based on Frank "Lefty" Rosenthal (see entry), who really did escape death from a car bomb.

Any Hot Springs around here?

Sure thing. Go to the Paradise Spa and Resort, they've got them there. It is on the Strip on the east side just past Mandalay Bay. Used to be a pretty nice place but it has fallen on hard times. B.t.w. Nevada is full of hot springs. There are several around Reno, some with bath houses. I used to sit in them by the hour. Especially the one by the Truckee River, pretty neat place. Reno gets very cold, you know.

Applegate-Lassen Cut-Off

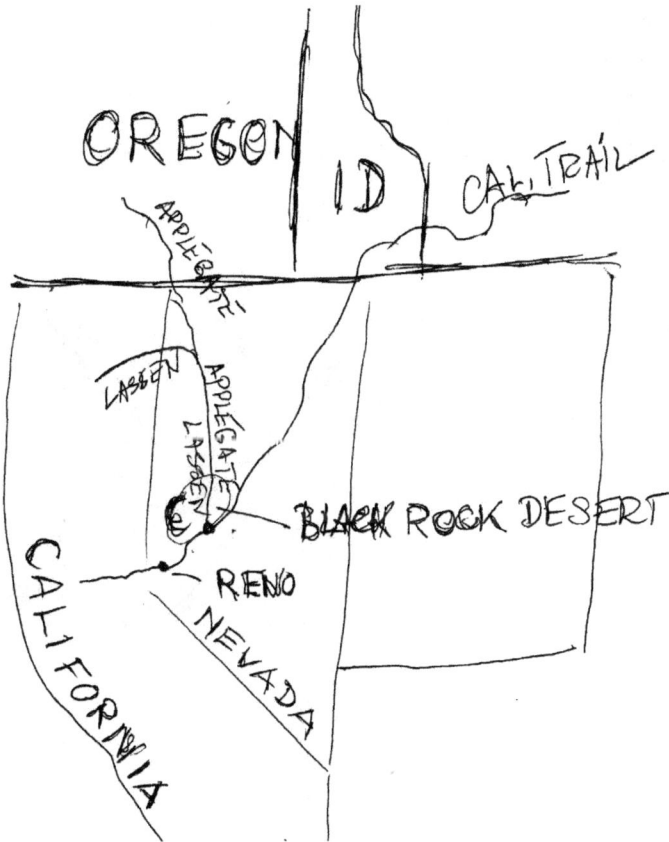

Developed by Danish immigrant Peter Lassen. Was a shortcut on the Old Emigrant Trail going into California. The 49ers initially made their way up the Humboldt River from the East Bay. Were they surprised when that river disappeared into the Humboldt sink! No more water! The cut-off crossed the Black Rock Desert in Nevada and continued into the gold fields of California. It was considered a very difficult shortcut. The Applegate trail paralleled the Lassen trail but veered north into Oregon.

Armpit of America

See Battle Mountain.

Area 51

North of Las Vegas, in the desert somewhere. Stealth fighters, aliens etc. We have heard the rumors, seen the movies (Men in Black etc.) If you want to have some fun and have a lot of time, drive up to Beatty on Route 95. They have a whole cottage industry having to do with aliens, flying saucers and space cadets.

Arrowhead Trail

This was an early automobile route between Salt Lake City and Los Angeles, California. It had the same logo that was used by the old Salt Lake, Los Angeles and San Pedro Railroad. Parts of the trail had different designations later on. U.S. 91, SR 6, Las Vegas Boulevard, and Fifth Street were some of the roads that used the same general routing.

Atomic Survival Town

Ruins of a town that was used in atomic testing.

The Atomic City
The buildings were used to test their
resistance to an atomic explosion.

Atomic Testing Museum

The only museum of its kind is at 755 East Flamingo Road in Las Vegas.

A Tough Sheriff

Ralph Lamb, sometimes called "the last cowboy sheriff," served Clark County from 1961 to 1979, the longest lasting tenure of any sheriff of the county. When he joined the force Clark County had a grand total of 15,000 residents (compared to over 2 million today). He never had any formal law enforcement training and worked his way up through the ranks. He passed away in 2015. He was never afraid to tackle the mob and mafia guys that were running the casinos at the time. In the end, because of his limited authority as a sheriff, he had to make accommodations and let a lot of things slide. Things changed after the Kefauver hearings in Congress and the FBI was sent in to clean things up.

Austin

ST. AUGUSTINE'S

Austin's oldest church, St. Augustine's, requires the bells in the tower to be rung by pulling a rope located in the men's restroom. The geographic center of Nevada is 26 miles southeast of Austin. The city has a population of 192 and sits at the junction of U.S. 50 and State Route 305. Many of the original buildings are still standing. It boasts of a few oldest, amongst them the oldest continually published paper, the Reese River Reveille, and the oldest bank building in Nevada.

A Watery Grave

In 1945 a B-29 bomber crashed and sank in Lake Mead in 300 feet of water. With the drought of the 2000's, that water was down to about 125 feet deep in 2015, and the crash site has become a favorite diving spot.

Bad Language

In a certain Nevada town it is against the law to use bad language in front of a dead body.

Bars and Churches

There are seven times more bars than there are churches in Nevada.

Battle at Pyramid Lake

NUMAGA

In 1860 white settlers raped some Paiute Indian girls. The Indians then started to slash and burn white settlers. Major William M. Ormsby (Ormsby County) got together a militia numbering about 105. They encountered a fate similar to the one suffered by a certain George Custer. In other words most of them got killed, including their glorious leader on May 12, 1860. They had made the same fatal mistake, namely overestimating their own ability and underestimating the enemy. The regular army was called in from San Francisco and on June 2, 1860 the battle was joined. The Indians were forced into the Black Rock Desert and a fort was built (Fort Churchill near present day Fallon).

FORT CHURCHILL

Battle Mountain

WOVOKA

In central Nevada, site of the largest major clash in the West between Indians and white settlers. Connected with the so-called "Ghost Dance" uprising. Wovoka was their charismatic spiritual leader. The town became notorious when USA Today called it the "armpit of America". That spawned the annual "Armpit Festival" sponsored by, who else, a deodorant manufacturer.

Beckwourth Pass

JIM BECKWOURTH

Jim Beckwourth was an African-American who was a famous scout/mountain man in the old west. This route is North of Reno and goes from there into California.

Berlin

BERLIN, NV

BERLIN, GERMANY

Yes, there is a Berlin in Nevada.

It is in central Nevada, pretty hard to reach and remote. But, it has a lot to offer. You have your ghost town, which is surprisingly well preserved. It may be because park rangers are on duty. They have the only complete skeleton of an Ichthyosaurus in the U.S. If you want to visit it is advisable to carry water, camping gear, and to use a four wheel drive vehicle with good ground clearance. The nearest town is two hours away by car.

Berlin Wall

An entrepreneur brought pieces of the Berlin Wall to Las Vegas and installed them behind a urinal at the Main Street Station Hotel and Casino.

Big Money

LIBERACE

Liberace got paid $300,000 a week for performing at the Las Vegas Hilton in the 1970's.

Biggest Gift Shop

The Bonanza gift shop at the corner of Sahara and the Strip claims to be the largest in the world.

Bing Crosby

Bing Crosby owned a couple of ranches in Nevada.

Black Book

Try not to get listed in this book. It'll get you barred from all Nevada casinos.

Black Mailbox

It can be found near Alamo. This is where mail for Area 51 and for alien hunters winds up. It is on Route 375, which almost runs parallel to Nellis Air Force Base. There are actually two reinforced boxes which get constantly vandalized. The box was stolen in January of 2015 and may not be replaced.. If you have alien mail send it to:

Mail Box Road, Alamo, NV 89001

Black Rock Desert

BLACK ROCK DESERT

North of Reno. Site of the annual "Burning Man Festival.."

Blue Diamond

The Blue Diamond mine close to Las Vegas had 99% pure gypsum. It closed in 1953.

Blue Jeans

Were invented in Reno by one Jacob Davis.

Bob Haslam and the Long Ride

Among all Pony Express Riders "Pony Bob" Haslam was a legend. Haslam gained fame for the enormous distance he covered while working for the Pony Express. He received the eastbound mail at Friday's Station, to be delivered to Buckland's Station. Arriving at that station the next rider was so frightened about Indian attacks he refused to accept the mail and to deliver. So Bob rode on, all the way to Smith's Creek. The entire ride covered 190 miles without a rest. After a rest of about eight hours Bob took the return mail bag with the westbound mail and began to retrace his ride. When he got to Cold Springs he discovered it had been raided by Indians, stock and supplies were gone, and the station master had been killed. Bob then kept riding until he reached Buckland's Station. The total distance covered was 380 miles, a truly amazing feat. Even in a car it is a good distance.

Bonnie and Clyde Death Car

Those two characters went on a crime spree back in the early 20th century. For some time they roamed the country robbing, stealing and murdering. When finally cornered by the Feds a gun fight ensued. They were both killed and their bullet-riddled car can now be viewed in the little town of Primm at the I-15 from California to Las Vegas. That town is little more than gambling places, a few hotels, a shopping mall and a gas station. There is a golf course also.

Boot Hill

Many mining towns had a boot hill. The best known one is in Virginia City.

Bowers Mansion

Not too far from Reno near Washoe Lake. Bowers was a mining magnate out of Virginia City where he made a tremendous amount of money. He built the mansion and took off for Europe with his wife. He returned after a few years with a boatload of antiques. Shortly thereafter he went broke and died in poverty. He and his wife are buried behind their mansion.

Boulder City

20 miles from Las Vegas en route to Hoover Dam. The only municipality in the State of Nevada without legal gambling. No slot machines, no bingo, no card games, no nothing. Gambling in the State is a LOCAL option. Oddly enough, with about 209 square miles it is the largest city by area in Nevada by far. Greater Las Vegas only occupies about 136 square miles. Reno comes in third with 106 square miles. The 2014 census set the Boulder City population at about 15,000. Boulder City also boasts a "haunted hotel," the old Boulder Dam Hotel.

Borax

About forty tons of Borax was shipped to San Pedro, California, to be converted to soap and detergent. A prominent spokesperson for the fourteen mule team Borax Co. was president Ronald Reagan with his show "Death Valley Days." Some large borax mines were located in Death Valley.

Boundary Peak

This is the highest peak in Nevada. Its elevation is about 13,000 feet. The odd thing (one of many odd things in Nevada) is that the peak was originally in California. The 1870 "von Schmidt" survey placed it in Esmeralda County, Nevada. There had been a boundary dispute around Lake Tahoe and von Schmidt surveyed the boundary line which was then .disputed. Only twenty years later a new survey moved the state line 20 miles west again. The von Schmidt boundary monument is around Needles, California near the Colorado River.

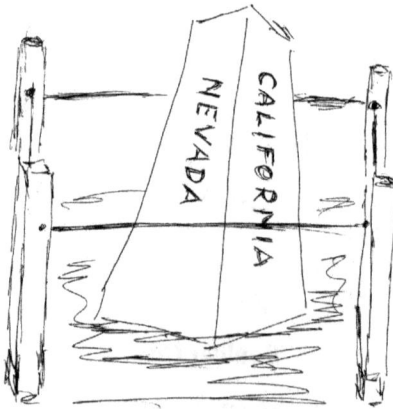

Bowling

If you like bowling go ahead and rent the KingPin suite at the Palms hotel. It has two fully functioning bowling alleys. Striiiike!

Bowling Scoring Display

The largest scoring display for bowling in the world is at the bowling center in Reno.

Boxing

GANS VS NELSON

The boxing match of Joe Gans vs. Battling Nelson took place on Labor Day, September 2, 1906. The fight lasted an astounding 45 rounds, something unheard of these days. The fight was decided by a low blow. In 1910 Nevada was the only state with legalized boxing.

Bradley House

Speaking about Boulder City (above), Mr. and Mrs. Bradley were the only African-Americans permitted to live in Boulder City in the 1930's. Even the Federal Government did not want them there. Their employer, Mr. Glover Ruckstell, owner of Grand Canyon Airlines, wanted them to stay there and backed them to the hilt. Mr. Bradley was the driver for Grand Canyon Tours and Mrs. Bradley prepared the lunches. They were originally from the Carolinas. This was the time of discrimination, and Nevada was as bad as any southern state.

Their original house is now in the Clark County Museum awaiting restoration. It started out as the ticket booth at the old Boulder City airport and has only 450 square feet. I don't know how those folks survived the brutal summer heat in that building.

Brahma Shrine

The Thai version of a Brahma Shrine is at Caesars Palace, behind the Serendipity restaurant. It is a Phra Phrom, and the only one in the Western Hemisphere. It is small.

Bren Tower

At the Nevada Test Site. Erected to simulate the radiation of the Hiroshima bomb. It also is one of the largest objects ever to have been relocated.

Bristlecone Pines

At Boundary Peak and other areas are the oldest living things (non-cloned) on earth; up to 4,000 years old.

Bunkerville

MR. BUNKERS FAMILY

Allegedly named via a coin toss between the two town founders Messrs. Leavitt and Bunker. Leavitt died at age 78 leaving behind five wives and 55 children. Bunker had three wives and 22 children when he passed away at age 79.

Bulldozer Games

They let you play with bulldozers and power shovels off Rancho Drive in Las Vegas. It is between Sirius and Meade. There is an hourly fee.

Burning Moscow

A mine in Virginia City.

Butch Cassidy

Butch Cassidy

On September 19, 1900, a bank robbery occurred in Winnemucca, and Butch Cassidy was accused of pulling off that heist. It turned out Butch could not have committed that crime because he was in Wyoming, performing another robbery. However, it is believed that three members of the Hole in the Wall gang were the culprits.

Caliche

Some people call it hardpan. It is a layer of soil underlying Las Vegas. It is extremely hard—I know, I had to use a pick to remove some from my yard. Water and plant roots find it very difficult to penetrate this layer. So, if you see a nice garden or lawn in Las Vegas think of the work that has gone into it. On the other hand, don't be too harsh on those folks that do not have a nice garden or lawn. Things are mighty tough around here for gardeners.

Caliente

The town by that name was first called Dutch Flat.

California Trail

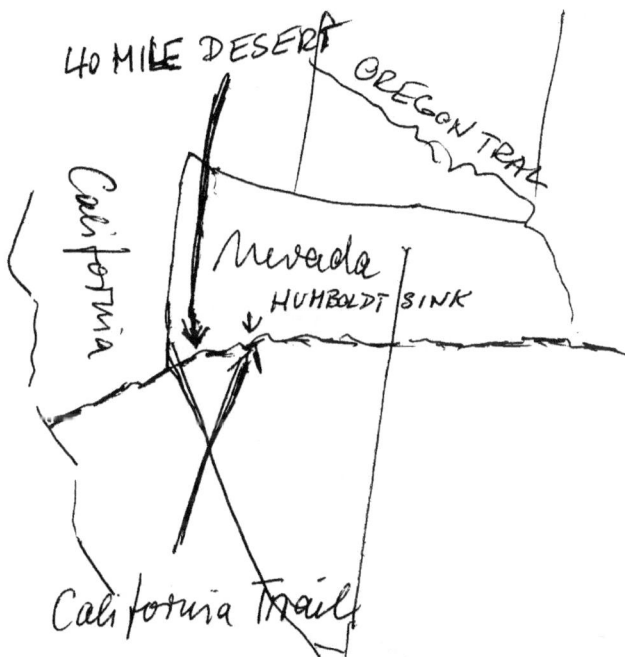

40 MILE DESERT — OREGON TRAIL — California — Nevada — HUMBOLDT SINK — California Trail

An estimated 300,000 persons made the journey from various points in Missouri to California. St. Joe was their jumping off point. The trail has numerous side spurs and cut-offs but hundreds of miles of wagon ruts are still visible in northern Nevada, mainly around Elko in the eastern part of the state

CalNevAri

A small town off Highway 95 south of Boulder City. It is California, Nevada and Arizona abbreviated.

Camels

Were used until 1870 for transport and freighting in the Nevada desert. The Camel Corps was authorized by Congress in 1855 and a certain Lt. Edward F. Beale was put in charge. The experiment failed but several of the camels did service as beasts of burden until 1870. They hauled freight from Sacramento, California, including salt and other supplies.

Camp Ely

CAMP ELY

A Pony Express station about ten miles south of Pioche. It was later renamed Bullionville.

Canals

Las Vegas has them at the Venetian Hotel, complete with singing gondoliers.

Candelaria

A town named after a Catholic Christmas holiday, "Candlemas."

Captain J.C. Fremont

Explored parts of the West on behalf of the U. S. Government. Discovered Pyramid Lake some 50 miles East of Reno.

Carp

The town of Carp is not named after a fish, but after a person. It is a railroad stop only.

Carson City

Smallest state capital in the U.S. It is so small that administration of the City and County was combined some years ago to save on expenses. It is in Douglas County. And yes, Kit Carson was here. It also was formerly an important location of the U.S. Mint. The famous "CC" silver dollars were minted here. The Mint is now a museum and the silver dollars (also called cartwheels) are collector's items. When I was a young guy those silver dollars could be found in all Nevada casinos. Large trays of them. Carson City also is one of two state capitals to adjoin another state, California. That shiny dome on the State Capitol building is a mixture of silver and other metals.

Cemeteries

In Reno, ten of them are on the list of historic places.

Champagne Stage Coach Robber

CHARLES BOLES

Charles Boles, AKA "Black Bart," staged several stagecoach robberies at or near the Geiger Grade, a road to Virginia City from Reno. Always very polite and genteel, he treated his victims to a glass of champagne after taking their money and before leaving the scene. He was caught in San Francisco because of a left-behind handkerchief that had a laundry mark. All in all he staged 27 robberies in California and Nevada to support his opulent lifestyle.

Charles Frey

A German immigrant living in San Francisco, California invented the first slot machine in 1899. He called it the Liberty Bell.

Cheating

Where there are casinos there are cheaters also. I would not recommend it. In the old days there was a certain casino in downtown Las Vegas that would have their security people take cheaters into their back alley and have them roughed up. I don't know if those stories are true but I have heard them many times from different people. If caught you could wind up in the Black Book, a list of unwanted people.

Chinese Immigrants

At the time of statehood, Chinese residents outnumbered persons of European ancestry five to one.

Chinatown

By 1878 Chinese immigrants who had been working on the railroad had established a community at First Street and Virginia in Reno. That year a fire of unknown origin erupted and destroyed some 50 homes. Some fingers were pointed at the Workingman's Party, but guilt was never established. In 1908 Chinatown was burned to the ground on orders of the Reno City Council for sanitary reasons. Some say it was burned down because it occupied a prime piece of property, coveted by some white folks.

City

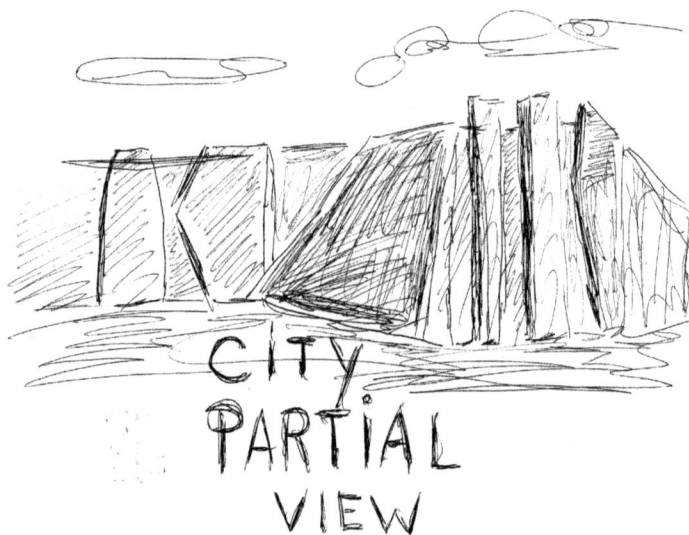

CITY PARTIAL VIEW

A large, if not the largest, sculpture ever built in modern times is in Hiko, a small town in Lincoln County. The artist, Michael Heizer, has been building it since 1972. He finances this effort by arranging art exhibits where he sells his art around the country. The structure being built stretches for almost a mile. There is a movement afoot to declare it a National Monument. Access is restricted by the reclusive artist. He previously constructed the "Double Negative," a series of trenches intersecting a canyon near Overton, Nevada. For that one he moved an estimated 200,000 tons of earth. Other large sculptures by other artists can be found in Utah including "Spiral Jetty" (by Robert Smithson), and in Arizona, near Flagstaff, "Roden Crater" (by James Turrell).

Clown Motel

CLOWN MOTEL
TONOPAH

That little gem can be found in Tonopah, about a hundred miles north of Las Vegas. I have heard good reports about it. Everything is clown in that place. The really odd thing is that it is sitting next to a long abandoned cemetery.

Chocolate

Chocolate lovers are in luck in Las Vegas (technically Henderson). The Ethel M chocolate factory is located on Sunset Road. The adjoining cactus garden is worth a visit all by itself.

Columbus

COLUMBUS

ESMERALDA COUNTY

Columbus is a ghost town in Esmeralda County. It had an explosive but brief history. In 1865 a quartz mill was established, in 1871 borax was discovered, in 1875 it had 1,000 inhabitants, in 1881 there were 100 people left. Fairly typical of the Nevada mining boom towns.

Comstock Lode

Nevada was made famous by the discovery of the Comstock Lode, the richest known U.S. silver deposit, in 1859. It also created several multi millionaires and helped to bring San Francisco on the map. The original prospectors were looking not for silver, but for gold.

Creech Air Force Base

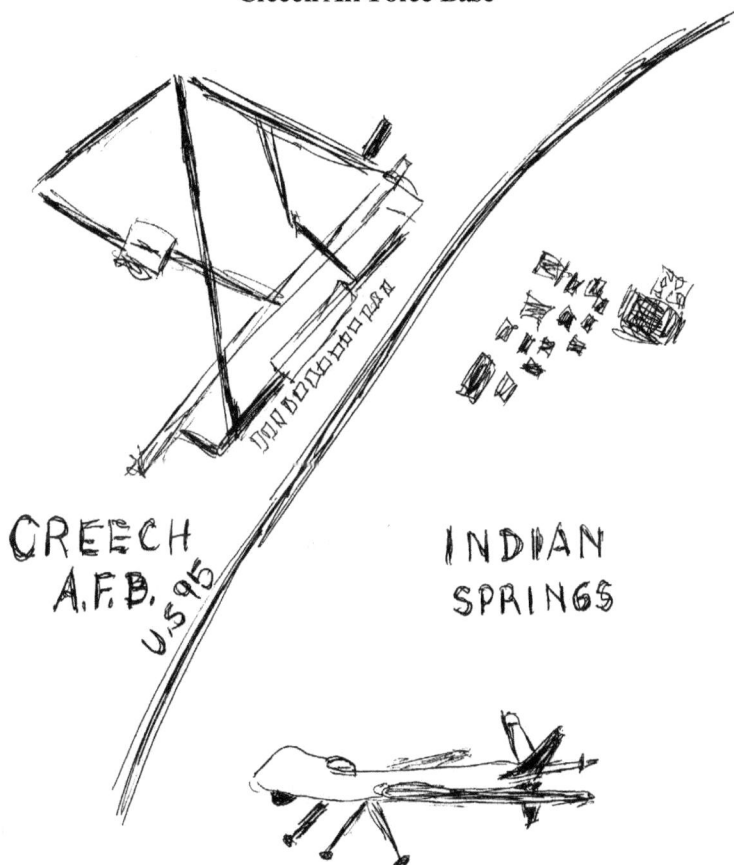

CREECH
A.F.B.
US 95

INDIAN
SPRINGS

Indian Springs Air Force Base is the former name of this location. It served as an aerial gunnery school during World War II. Now spooks use it for drone control.

Cui-Ui

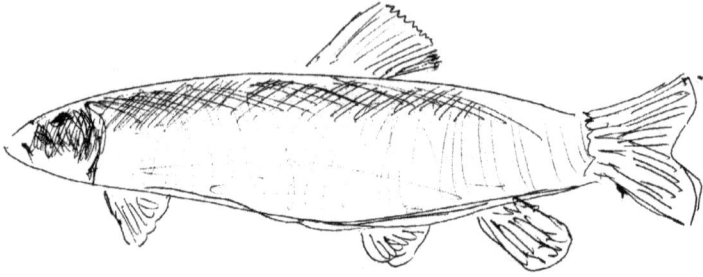

The Cui-Ui is a prehistoric fish residing in Pyramid Lake, east of Reno.

Culinary Local 226

One of the largest Unions of its kind in the U.S. Around 35,000 members at the moment and growing. Al Bramlet was the genius behind it.

THE COMBINATION SHAFT
VIRGINIA CITY, NV

Deep Shaft

One of the deepest mine shafts in the world is located in Virginia City, Nevada in the Comstock Lode. The shaft is well over 3,000 feet deep and almost as deep as the deepest shaft in the world, the Adalbert Shaft in Joachimstal, Bohemia. Mine shafts in the Comstock Lode were so deep, miners could work only 30 minutes at a time because of the heat. It is reported that temperatures in the mines reached 130 degrees. Most of the miners died young. Dust would get into their lungs and would make the inside of the lungs resemble a rock (silicosis). Life expectancy was about 40 years of age. The ones that made the real money were the mine owners and the bar owners and merchants who supplied the mines. Don't get me wrong, the miners were highly paid for the time, more than any other trade. It was the working conditions that did them in. The above described shaft (the Combination Shaft) wasn't the only deep shaft in Virginia City. Several others were around 3,000 feet, but none was as deep as the Combination Shaft. The estimated length of all the tunnels is about 100 miles.

Dat-So-La-Lee

Is the name of the famous basket weaver of the Washoe Native Americans. Her baskets are so finely crafted they are now in the Smithsonian Institution.

Delta Saloon

The Delta Saloon is in Virginia City. I am mentioning it here because it has on display the suicide table. A gambler lost all his money playing Faro and committed suicide right there at the table. For an explanation about the game check the Faro entry.

Dentures

In Las Vegas it is illegal to pawn your own dentures.

Desert Tortoise

The desert tortoise spends most of its life underground to escape the hot days and cold nights of the typical Nevada desert. It can live to be 70 years old.

Desert Triangles

The Desert Triangles are located not too far away from downtown Las Vegas. They are quite large, about 950 feet by 1,700 feet. They were used to train gunners for the U.S. Army Air Force and were located at their Gunnery School, now Nellis Air Force Base. More than 45,000 B-17 gunners were trained at the site. I know of no way to go to those triangles via ground transport, as they are inside a Nellis A.F.B. shooting range. Best viewing would be from the air.

Devil's Hole Pupfish

It is a tiny fish that lives in the Devil's Hole in the Ash Meadows Wildlife Refuge. There are only a few of them and it is endangered.

Dice

Las Vegas casino dice have no rounded corners and have ID numbers.

Donner Party/Ranch/Trail/Pass

A sad tale of hunger, death, cannibalism and survival. The Donner Pass crosses the Sierra Nevada close to Reno. The Donner Trail is the route through the Donner Pass, and the Donner Party was a group of 49ers that got stuck there in 40 feet of snow and resorted to eating one another to survive. The Donner Ranch, situated outside Verdi, Nevada near Reno was the jumping off point for many wagon trains trying to cross the mountains. It is ideally located near a bend of the Truckee River which flows from Lake Tahoe to Pyramid Lake. I was a chef at that ranch for a while in the sixties when it was one of many divorce ranches in Nevada.

Double Negative

Is a sculpture entrenched in earth. It is one of the largest sculptures on earth. About 240,000 tons of rhyolite and sandstone were blasted away and carried away to create it. It is now owned by the Museum of Contemporary. Art in Los Angeles. It was created in 1969 by Michael Heizer and his helpers. It is 1,500 feet long, 30 feet wide and 50 feet deep. It lies near the small town of Overton, about 80 miles northeast of Las Vegas. Well worth the trip, not only to see it but also to get a glimpse of rural Nevada. The artist has by now been working for thirty (yes 30) years on a project a mile long called "City." It is also in Nevada but northwest of Cedar City, Utah. Allegedly it is visible on Google Earth.

Dragons

Nevada is the only state to possess a complete skeleton—approximately 55 feet long—of an Ichthyosaur, an extinct marine reptile.

Drinks

In Nyala a man is forbidden from buying drinks for more than three people other than himself at any one period during the day. The town was formerly called Mormon Well and is located in Nye county.

Ducks

Nevada's State artifact is the Tule Duck which was created nearly 2,000 years ago. Discovered by archeologists in 1924 during an excavation at Lovelock Cave, the 11 decoys are each formed of a bundle of bull rush (tule) stems, bound together and shaped to resemble a canvasback duck.

Dry

Nevada is the driest state in the nation. Some areas receive less than four inches of rain per year.

Dymaxion Car

One of three originals is housed in Reno, in the National Car Museum. Developed by Buckminster Fuller, architect and inventor of the geodesic dome, it was an aerodynamic, three-wheeled, 1930's car prototype meant to eventually lead to a flying car.

Earth Curvature

At the Bonneville Salt Flats, at a grotto of boulders overlooking the flats it is possible to observe the curvature of the earth. Only a few places in the U.S. offer that view.

Elephant Rock

ELEPHANT ROCK

A sandstone rock formation that can be found in the Valley of Fire state park.

Elko

Lowell Thomas called it "the last cow town in America." The annual cowboy poetry/song gathering takes place here.

Elvis Presley

He performed 837 consecutive shows at the Las Vegas Hilton. All of them were sold out. His glittery white jumpsuit lives on in a glass display case, as do several hundred impersonators.

Ely

Ely in northern Nevada is the location of the largest glory hole in the Western Hemisphere. This large hole in the ground was created through the removal of copper ore. The mine is long since defunct. The ore was taken by a short haul railroad to a nearby smelter. Some years ago there was some effort to keep this line as a tourist attraction. It is also one of only three places in the U.S. where three interstate highways converge.

"Enola Gay"

From 1941 to 1977 the U.S. Army Air Force and then the U.S. Air Force had a bombing training facility at Wendover Air Force Base, Nevada (there is a Wendover, Utah also). Crews for B-17, B-24 and B-29 planes were trained. The Enola Gay was stationed there with one of the bombing groups. In case you forgot or never knew, the Enola Gay was the B-29 that dropped the first atomic bomb on Hiroshima on August 6, 1945. The Enola Gay hangar and museum are located on the base, which is now a civilian airport. All in all twenty-one bombardment groups were trained at the base which has almost ideal flying conditions. Wendover itself started as a service stop for the Union Pacific Railroad. Not too far away, inside the state of Utah is the spot where the U.P and the Central Pacific Railroad joined up in the 1840's. Also nearby are the Bonneville salt flats that are used from time to time for land speed records.

Eureka

Eureka County has seven communities with a combined population of about 2,000, but it has an area of over 4,000 square miles. Eureka, the county seat, has a scant 600 inhabitants.

Forty-Mile Desert

Part of the Old Emigrant Trail to California, a great obstacle for the 49ers on their way west. It is said that for many years after 1849 this desert was strewn with discarded household objects and the remains of animals that had died trying to cross this burning desert in the middle of the summer. Travel agents back east did not tell (or did not know) about this piece of territory.

Faro

Also called "bucking the tiger" for obvious reasons. A fast moving, simple to learn card game that once was very popular across the U.S. and other countries. It was so popular during the Civil War there were no less than 150 Faro halls in Washington D.C. I am not aware of any faro halls in Las Vegas. It has gone away together with Panguingue.

First Airplane

The first airplane to land in Las Vegas was piloted by Mr. Beckley. There is a large display at McCarran Airport about it. Interesting stuff. It is at the departure level.

First Casino

The Pair-O-Dice in 1931 on Highway 91, now called the Strip.

First Lady

PAT NIXON

The only First Lady from Nevada was Pat Nixon. Pat Nixon was born Thelma Catherine Ryan in 1912 in Ely, White Pine County.

First Mayor

PETE BUOL

Las Vegas, Peter Buol, 1911-1913.

First Europeans

TRAPPER

The first recorded European men in the Elko area were fur trappers who trapped beaver in the area starting in 1823.

Fifteenth Amendment

Nevada was the first state to ratify the Voting Rights Amendment.

First Trading Post

The first trading post was established by Howard Beatie in June of 1850 in Carson Valley. He was the first European settler in the area.

Floor Numbers

Las Vegas hotels have no floor 13. Some of them do not have a floor number 4, because it is an Asian bad luck number.

Fort Ruby

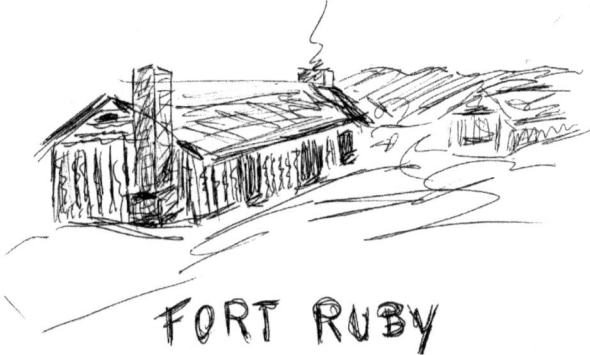

FORT RUBY

Also known as Camp Ruby, it was built during the Civil War to protect the Overland Mail and the Pony Express. It was built in 1861 and served until 1869. It is located in White Pine County.

Frank "Lefty" Rosenthal

FRANK ROSENTHAL "LEFTY"

He was the sports book odds maker at the now defunct Stardust Hotel/Casino. He is widely credited as the inventor of the modern sports book. He was also a mathematical genius, able to remember the odds on dozens of sports teams. He ran afoul of someone in Las Vegas and left town in a hurry after his car got blown up.

Fly Ranch Geyser

Created by drillers looking for water. It was supposed to play out after a few days. Well, it has been a few years now, (fifty plus) and the colorful deposits around it keep getting higher, a real tourist attraction.

FLY RANCH GEYSER

Gambling

A 1910 law made it illegal to gamble in Las Vegas. In 1931, a gambling bill was approved that made gambling legal again.

Gambling is Nevada's prime source of income, averaging around 75% of the state's annual revenue. Mining is the second source, tourism the third. But, according to the latest figures, shopping and entertainment may have overtaken gambling as the main source of income.

Gandy Dancer

It is a person who walks between railroad tracks on orders of the railroad owners to look for loose spikes and other irregularities. A boring job in Nevada.

Giant Prospector

THE GIANT PROSPECTOR

Can be seen in Washoe Valley on the road from Reno to Carson City. There is another Giant Prospector in downtown Las Vegas.

Genoa

Oldest continually inhabited settlement in Nevada. About 300 people live there. It is really cute and picturesque. Visit it during their annual "Candy Dance" at the end of September, a benefit for the volunteer fire department. The little town of Dayton which is nearby periodically claims to be the oldest settlement. Genoa was a trading station along the Emigrant Trail to California and is home of Nevada's oldest bar, circa 1853, an authentic old west bar whose mirror was shipped from Scotland around the horn to San Francisco and thence to Genoa by covered wagon.

Goldfield, Gold Point, Gold Hill

GOLD FIELD   GOLD HILL

Goldfield is in Central Nevada off Route I-95, the Las Vegas to Reno Highway. Once one of the largest cities west of Chicago, now one of the smallest. Now the wind blows through tumbledown shacks. The Goldfield Hotel is a major, very large building from that period still standing. Gold Point is in the main compass direction, but off I-95. It is semi-deserted. This town is so isolated it did not receive telephone service until 1995. Imagine, those folks got by without a phone. Well, not really. All they had to do is to drive to the nearest town, Lida, and place calls from there. That phone was conveniently located inside a brothel. The town of Gold Point, on the other hand, is near Reno, about 25-30 miles south as the crow flies. Its claim to fame is the oldest hotel in Nevada that has been in continuous operation. Like so many other old places in the state, it has its resident ghosts.

Ghost Towns

There are literally hundreds of ghost towns all over Nevada. Most of them are nothing but a collection of foundation stones. A few remaining ones are substantial. Do not enter any abandoned mines or mine shafts! The ones I visited didn't have much to offer. Ever since those little all terrain vehicles came out the vandals have been all over.

60

Giant Flashlight

GIANT FLASHLIGHT

Created by Claes Oldenburg and Coosje van Bruggen, it is on display at the entrance of Artemus Ham Hall at UNLV on Maryland Parkway, in Las Vegas It was erected on March 11, 1981, is black and 38 feet tall.

Glaciers

The southernmost glacier in the U.S. is in the Great Basin National Park.

Goldwell Open Air Museum

This one is near the ghost town of Rhyolite., four miles west of Beatty, off State Highway 374. The figures represent the Last Supper.

Golden DeLorean

This car is at the Reno National Automobile Museum.

Gold Hill

In the 1860's Gold Hill rivaled Virginia City in size and population. It is only about a mile from Virginia City and at one time 8,000 folks called it home. Now there are about 200 still hanging on. The town also lays claim to the oldest hotel in Nevada still operating. It opened in 1861.

Gold Point

Formerly called Lime Point and Hornsilver. It is off U.S. 95 north of Beatty, in Esmeralda County. Some fifty old buildings are still standing. A few old timers still hang on, including the sheriff who also makes his home there. The town is short of water and it is trucked in via 255 gallon tanks. The outhouse is unusual in that it has two entrances, male and female.

Golden Trout

Only found in Nevada mountain lakes above 10,000 feet. If you are interested in catching these sport fish I would recommend the eastern part of the state. Try Elko and go from there to Lamoille Canyon. Make local inquiries before leaving the main roads!!

Goodsprings

About 40 miles south of Las Vegas. I like to mention this town here because of the very odd Pioneer bar in that town. It is only a third of a bar. It was built in Maine around 1860, then shipped around the Horn in three sections. The first section was lost, the second section burned and the third section is what you see.

Great Basin National Park

As well as being home to the most southernmost glacier in the U.S., it is also the location of the Lehman Cave, one of the most extensive cave systems in the U.S.

Guru Road

GURU ROAD
GERLACH, NV

Between Gerlach and Empire. Filled with folk art for about one mile.

Hand of Faith

Enormous gold nugget resembling a hand. Found in Australia in someone's backyard. Can be seen in the Golden Nugget, downtown Las Vegas. It was found by Kevin Hiller in Victoria, Australia on September 26, 1980. using a metal detector. It weighs about 875 Troy ounces or about 27 Kg. It measures 47 cm x 20 cm x 9 cm. Larger nuggets were found, but this is the largest still around.

THE HAND OF FAITH NUGGET

Hanging Bridge

It is the bridge across the Truckee River at South Virginia Street in Reno. Sometime in the 1880's, crime was getting out of hand in Reno and the local constabulary (cops) wouldn't or couldn't do anything about it. The citizens formed a vigilante committee and posted fliers warning all "crossroaders," etc. to get out of town by the following morning. Some weren't fast enough and were hanged off the bridge. Word has it there may have been up to twelve bodies. Peace and quiet ensued.

Hard Hats

The Hoover Dam project was the first large scale construction project that required workers to wear hard hats. European and Bohemian miners had worn variants of hard hats long before that, but they were never a requirement. The first hats of that kind were made of leather. After World War I steel began to be used, and after that the sky was the limit.

Harrison House

1001 F Street, North Las Vegas. African-American performers were not allowed to stay in any hotel on the strip. After they made a lot of money for their employer they were shunted off to this boarding house, the only place for them to stay. Yes, Las Vegas was as segregated as any state in the south.

Heart Attacks

Those you can get at the Heart Attack Grill, on Fremont Street in downtown Las Vegas. The servers wear nurses' uniforms and carry first aid kits. Their biggest item is a "Butter Shake." Another is a burger so huge they will pay you if you can eat one. Their quadruple burger is listed at 9,982 calories. I could not find a caloric listing for the octuple burger, but based on the previous burger it should be around 20,000 calories. Their fries are cooked in lard and their buns are coated with lard. Their vegetarian menu consists of cigarettes. All burgers can be ordered with extra bacon—the octuple has 40 slices of bacon, and no sharing or splitting of orders.

Hawthorne Naval Ammunition Depot

One of the largest (US) naval munitions depots anywhere. Hundreds of miles from the ocean, in the middle of the desert. The town sits on the edge of a huge lake. That part of Nevada is really pretty on account of the lake and the tall mountains to the west of it.

Hemenway

It is the name of a boat ramp/harbor at Lake Mead. Nothing unusual about that. What is odd is the fact that no one seems to know where the name originated. Lake Mead isn't that old as lakes go. Nevada isn't that old either. But no one seems to know who/where/what about that name. If you happen to have some info on it let me know, please.

He saved his company

The CEO of FedEx saved the company by winning big at a Las Vegas blackjack table. The winnings allowed the company to pay the fuel bill.

Highest Grossing Entertainer

In 1999 Barbara Streisand pulled in almost $15,000,000 for a concert at the MGM Grand.

Highest Paid Entertainer

Liberace was paid an amazing $300,000 per week in the 1970's He appeared at the Hilton on Paradise Road, formerly the International.

Las Vegas Highest Temperature

118 degrees Fahrenheit in July 1931, almost 48 degrees Celsius.

Hole in the Wall Gang

Butch Cassidy

Butch Cassidy and the Sundance Kid staged a train robbery near Winnemucca at the beginning of the past century. He was later ruled out as one of the robbers, as he was robbing banks in Wyoming at the time. Butch Cassidy himself was born not that far away from Las Vegas, in Beaver, Utah. His real name was Parker.

Horses in Casinos

DO NOT RIDE YOUR HORSE INTO A HOTEL

After 1938 you could no longer bring saddled horses into a casino.

Horses

There are about 25,000 wild horses in Nevada.

Hotels

Of the 20 largest hotels in the world, 17 are in Las Vegas.

Hotel Rooms

Las Vegas has more hotel rooms than any other place (that we know of). It normally also has the highest occupancy rates. 95% occupancy is not unheard of.

Howard Hughes

In 1966, Howard Hughes began his infamous, reclusive stay at the Desert Inn. By 1968, Hughes purchased the Desert Inn after being asked to leave by hotel management.

You see the name Hughes on numerous locations and developments in Las Vegas. Howard Hughes bought up considerable Nevada property before he died in 1976, including the following hotels and casinos: Castaways, Desert Inn, Frontier, Landmark, Sands, Silver Slipper, and Harold's.

Humboldt River

The Humboldt is the largest river in Nevada, but it starts and ends all within the state's borders.

Humboldt Museum

Winnemucca.

I have the nuts

A good poker hand.

Implosions

Fifteen, yes, 15 casinos have been blown up or demolished in Las Vegas since 1993 to make room for new buildings. The next one to go as of this writing is the Riviera.

Dunes, October 22, 1993.

Landmark, November 7, 1995.

Sands, November 26, 1996.

Hacienda, January 1, 1997.

Aladdin, April 27, 1998.

El Rancho, October 3, 2000.

Desert Inn, October 23, 2001.

Castaways, January 11, 2006.

Bourbon Street, February 14, 2006.

Boardwalk, May 9, 2006.

Stardust, March 7, 2007.

New Frontier, November 13, 2007.

Clarion, February 10, 2015.

The Riviera.

I did not list the Harmon, the never-finished hotel on the Strip that was demolished because of construction defects. No implosion there. That one was dismantled, piece by piece, all 22 stories.

Indian Joe

Allegedly a Southern Paiute. Wanted for murder, he hid for years in caves along the Colorado River and was never caught. Some years later, bones and artifacts were found that were said to have belonged to him. So far as I can ascertain it was never proven.

Indian Springs

Was an aerial gunnery school during World War II. It now is Creech Air Force Base, home to the air force drone controllers.

Indoor Fun

The Scheel's sporting goods store in Sparks has an indoor display of 14 presidents. They are animatronic and speak as a person walks by. There also is a 40-foot tall Ferris wheel and an airplane hanging off the ceiling.

International Car Forest of the Last Church

Look for it near Goldfield, two hundred miles north of the Las Vegas Strip. Some forty cars were buried to make a sculpture garden.

Interstate 50

Is often called "the loneliest road in America." It stretches for 287 miles between Ely and Fernley with hardly a human in sight. Travelers are advised to carry water and extra gas.

Interstate 80

At 2,899 miles, I-80 is the second longest Interstate in the U.S. Through Nevada it passes through Fernley, Lovelock, Winnemucca, Battle Mountain, Elko, Wells and enters the state of Utah at West Wendover. Generally it follows portions of the California Trail, the First Transcontinental Railroad and the Feather River Route. In its entirety through the state it follows SR 1, the Victory Highway and U.S. 40.

Ione

This ghost town has a number of interesting buildings left standing. It is close to the other well preserved ghost town of Berlin. Again, this is a remote area. Ione was prominent during its heyday, but when the mines petered out the miners picked up and left.

JACK DEMPSEY

Jack Dempsey

Was the bouncer and bartender at the Mispah Hotel in Tonopah.

Jaguars

They show up from time to time at the southernmost point of the state, around Laughlin. There are about 12 of them and wildlife managers think they cross the Colorado river from Arizona.

Jarbidge

Is the first designated Wilderness Area, so designated in 1964. It is so remote only about three hundred people per year visit it. At 113,000 acres it is quite sizable, and includes mountains, forests and meadows.

Jiggs

Was named after a comic strip character that appeared in "Bringing up Father." This town is south of Elko. It formerly was named Hylton, Skelton and Mound Valley, ALL at the same time.

Jedediah Smith

Famous mountain man. He loved to travel and scouted the West extensively in the 1830's. He was killed by Indians in New Mexico at age 32. His original mission was to disrupt or destroy the British fur trade. He entered Nevada in1829.

John Roselli

Also called "Handsome Johnny," he was the mob enforcer at several Las Vegas Strip casinos. He was born July 4, 1905 and died August 8, 1976. His death was especially gruesome. His body was found decomposing in a 55 gallon steel drum, floating in Dumfounding Bay, Florida, near Miami.

Julia Bulette

A famous madam in Virginia City. She became very wealthy running a house of pleasure called Julie's Palace. Despite all of that she was very highly regarded in the community because of her charitable work. She literally helped hundreds of folks that had fallen on hard times. She donated large sums to the fire department and was made an honorary member of Engine Company 1. She was murdered on January 20, 1867 by drifter John Millain. On the day of her funeral the entire city closed down, mines, mills, saloons, bars, banks, all of it. Her funeral was attended by thousands, including Mark Twain. The Nevada Militia marched in the procession.

Kangaroo Rat

In Death Valley, the Kangaroo Rat can live its entire life without drinking a drop of liquid.

Kiel Ranch

Built in 1875 by Conrad Kiel, the ranch was the site of a gunfight and two murders by the end of the 19th century. It became a dude ranch and divorce ranch and was renamed the Boulderado Ranch and became quite popular.

Kirk Kerkorian and Howard Hughes

It may be just me but I see a lot of similarities between H.H. and K.K. Take the initials for instance. Both made their money in the airline business (TWA and Western), both were connected with films and film making (MGM and Republic), both owned (and own) casinos (Desert Inn, Landmark, Silver Slipper, Frontier for H.H., the Continental now Hilton, the MGM old and new for K.K.), both kept a low profile, both were filthy rich. What gives here? Mr. Kerkorian passed away in 2015 at age 98.

Krupp Ranch

Vera Krupp, a German actress who married and divorced the German munitions king Krupp, had a ranch in Red Rock Canyon during the 1950's and 60's. One of her prized possessions was a huge diamond ring. She was robbed of the ring by three men at gunpoint, right in her living room. It took a few weeks, but the police found the men and retrieved the disassembled ring. After the death of Vera Krupp the ring was put up for auction and none other than Richard Burton bought it for his wife Elizabeth Taylor in 1968 for $305,000, a large amount of money at the time.. The ranch is now state property and is called Spring Mountain Ranch State Park. It welcomes visitors.

Kit Carson

Yup, that famous old scout was here (Carson City). He was a lot like Washington that way, he slept everywhere. He also was the only illiterate Brigadier General in the U.S. Army. He learned to write his name only, but still preferred to sign with a thumbprint.

Lake Mead

Forty miles east of Las Vegas, it is the largest man-made body of water in the Western Hemisphere, some 115 miles in length. Good fishing and swimming. Don't expect any shade, there ain't none. It is the only lake with an outlet to the sea.

Lake Mead Carp

They are huge. Why doesn't anyone around here catch these as a food fish? In Eastern Europe, Poland especially, carp are grown commercially as a food fish.

Lake Tahoe

In Northern Nevada is the third deepest lake in North America, well over 1,500 feet. The only lakes deeper are Great Slave Lake and Crater Lake. The lake is actually divided between California and Nevada. Don't try to swim in it, it is very cold.

Land Sailing

Is a popular sport wherever there is a dry, smooth lake bed. One of those spots is Misfits Flat outside of Reno.

Largest Casino Floor

It is at the Venetian/Palazzo combined.

The single largest is at the Mandalay Bay.

Largest City

The largest city in land size is not Las Vegas or Reno. It is Boulder City which boasts a population of around 15,000 but has a land area of around 210 square miles. Greater Las Vegas is next with 136 square miles and Reno follows with 110 square miles.

Largest Climbing Wall

It is at the Basecamp Boulder Park in Reno and is 164 feet tall.

Large Counties

Of the ten largest counties in the U.S., three are located in Nevada.

1. Nye County – 18,000 square miles
2. Elko County – 17,000 square miles
3. Lincoln County – 10,600 square miles.

The largest county in the U.S. is San Bernardino in California, with about 20,000 square miles. Alaska has boroughs, not counties, otherwise those would be larger. Louisiana has no counties but parishes.

Nye County is so large, five states could fit into it.

Largest Hotels

Of the ten largest hotels in the world, six are located in Las Vegas:

1) Venetian-Palazzo – 7,117 rooms.

2) MGM Grand – 6,852 rooms.

6) Wynn-Encore – 4,750 rooms

7) Mandalay Bay-Delano – 4,426 rooms

8) Luxor – 4,408 rooms

10) Excalibur – 4,008 rooms.

Largest Jackpot

$39,713,982.25 was won by a software engineer from California at the Excalibur on March 21, 2003.

Largest Public Works Project

Hoover Dam was the largest ever in U.S. history.

Larger Size

Nevada is one of only two states to become much larger after admission to the Union. In 1866 a part of western Utah Territory was added to punish Utah for Mormonism. In January 1867 Nevada got a large piece of land added from Arizona Territory. Arizona had been suspected of aiding the Confederacy.

Lasers

In Henderson, a twin city to Las Vegas, it is against the law to aim a laser at someone's eyes.

Last Stage Coach Robber

When Ben Kuhl robbed a stage coach he became the first person in the U.S. convicted by the use fingerprints. Ben robbed the stage in Jarbidge, a very remote area. His life reads almost like a western movie. He lived for eight years with Indians, killed an outlaw at age 16, fought Pancho Villa, became a famous cowboy, got injured in World War I, and later became a successful movie actor. It doesn't get better than this.

Las Vegas Location

The site was chosen because it is midway between Los Angeles and Salt Lake City and had abundant well water at the time, which made it an ideal stop for trains. Locomotives needed water. It was the Los Angeles, San Pedro and Salt Lake Railroad. Las Vegas is Spanish for "the Meadows," which is also a place name you see around town, but the meadows have now dried up.

Las Vegas Beginning

The city was founded May 15, 1905.

Las Vegas Sign

The "Welcome to Fabulous Las Vegas" sign was never design protected. It was designed by Betty Willis, a designer working for Young Electric Sign Company, in one afternoon in 1959. The circles behind the words Las Vegas represent silver dollars. The company is still in existence and is responsible for many of the glitzy neon-tubed, light covered facades at the casinos. Incidentally, if you think they're wasting energy, most of those signs have gone to LED lighting.

Las Vegas Boulevard

The boulevard has had a few prior names. The locals call it the Strip, but it was also called, at one time or the other Arrowhead Trail, SR 6, U.S. 91, and let's not forget 5th Street.

LaVere Redfield

Here is a life story so unique I had to include it here. He was born in poverty in Ogden, Utah, and moved to California where he made a fortune during the depression buying distressed property and bankrupt oil companies. He was notoriously thrifty, even to the point of parking his truck on an incline because the battery was gone. He let it roll down and popped the clutch to get it started. I lived in Reno at the time and drove by his house many times. His capers are legendary. He once got $50,000 in silver coins from a bank. He returned all of them because the bank wanted to charge him $10 for the bags. In 1952 seven robbers stole his safe with $1.5 million in cash, jewelry and stock certificates. The police were able to apprehend the robbers and return all but $150,000 of the stolen money. But now the IRS had heard of the case and asked him about the origin of all that wealth. They took him to court for tax evasion. He was a little bit too thrifty and served as his own attorney, he did not want to pay for one. He lost the case, got fined $60,000 and did 18 months in jail. He got out on 1962. In 1963 he was the victim of another burglary. While in prison he got a free gall bladder operation. He died in 1974. After his death the real fireworks started when his estate became public. It turned out he owned 500 sections—that's right, sections, not acres—of prime land around Washoe county, mostly timber. The IRS found 680 bags of precious metal and gold coins behind false walls made of cardboard and concrete. There were no less than 407,283 Morgan and Peace dollars, 351,259 of them uncirculated.

Lenin

A large statue of Lenin is in front of the Russian dinner house at Mandalay Bay in Las Vegas. It is on the left as you enter from the parking garage. Someone chopped off the head because they dislike communists, but it has been known to reappear from time to time.

Lightly Traveled

State Route 266 is used by less than 50 vehicles per day. The road runs from U.S. 95 to the California line via Lida for about 40 miles. Lida is just another ghost town and, at an elevation of better than 6,000 feet, it gets pretty cold. The whole place is privately owned.

Licking Cat Head

This giant cat head sculpture sits at the corner of Coolidge Avenue and South First Street in Las Vegas. It was designed by Jesse Smigel and he named it "Snowball." It was installed in 2014 and stands ten feet tall.

Little A'Le'Inn

An eatery on the Extraterrestrial Highway. Caters to those who think aliens are among us.

Little Finland

Sunburst Arch
Little Finland

A geological oddity in Clark County, Nevada. Scientists think it is a frozen sandstorm. A lot of odd rock formations can be seen here.

Longest Running Show

The Folies Bergere at the Tropicana opened in 1959.

Looooong!

The longest telegram in Morse code ever sent was the Nevada constitution in 1864 from Carson City to Washington, D.C. Lincoln was in somewhat of a hurry to get Nevada admitted on account of the Civil War. It took two days, October 26 and 27, to transmit, had 16,543 words, and cost $4,303.27. That was an enormous amount in those days. It resulted in getting Nevada admitted as an anti-slavery state.

Lots of Cats

The MGM has an indoor lion display. The Mirage has an indoor tiger display.

Lots of Concrete

Enough concrete was used in Hoover Dam to pave a two lane road from San Francisco to New York City.

Lots of Explosions

From 1951 to 1992, 928 atomic tests took place at the Nevada Test Site.

Lots of Fish

The Mandalay Bay hotel has an indoor aquarium, the Golden Nugget has an indoor aquarium, the Silverton has an indoor aquarium, the Bellagio has an indoor aquarium, and the Mirage has an indoor aquarium.

Lots of Ribs

The "Best in the West" annual rib cook off in Sparks attracts 500,000 customers, and 200,000 pounds of ribs are prepared.

Lots of Slots

Nevada allows slot machines at airports, bars and grocery stores.

Lovelock

Is the home of the Nevada State Prison and also the home of a certain O. J. Simpson. (as of this writing).

Lowest Nevada Temperature Ever

Minus 50 degrees was recorded on January 8, 1937 in San Jacinto, Elko County.

Lunar Crater

This landscape feature is in a very remote location, 70 miles east-northeast of Tonopah, in Nye County. It is a designated National Natural Landmark. I don't know if it's worth a trip, although it is over 400 feet deep. It is an extinct volcano.

Mark Twain

Started his writing career at the Virginia City Territorial Enterprise as a reporter. He went on to become quite famous with such classics as "The Famous Jumping Frogs of Calaveras County," "Innocents Abroad," "Huckleberry Finn," and others. Calaveras County is just across the line from Nevada in California. The Mark Twain Museum is located at 47-53 South C Street, Virginia City. The other famous writer on that paper was Dan DeQuille.

Marshall Caifano

He was a high ranking member of the "Chicago Outfit," a Mafia gang. He changed his name to John Marshall after he arrived in Las Vegas on orders from Chicago, to keep an eye on Mafia controlled casinos. He was a suspect in more than ten gangland slayings. While in

Florida he was convicted for transporting stolen securities and did ten years in prison. He died in 2003.

McKeeversville

Originally an illegal squatters' camp, now a part of Boulder City called "Lakeview." It does have a good view of the lake. In the old days this was just a bunch of tents and huts. No one had any title to any of the land. And, it existed before Boulder City came into being.. There were some plans in the past to kick out the squatters but it seems no one wanted the political fallout. The town still exists to this day.

Million Dollar Courthouse

It is situated in the now very small town of Pioche, about 180 miles northeast of Las Vegas. This building, begun in 1871, was estimated to cost about $30,000 to construct. After some creative financing and influence peddling it wound up costing over $1,000,000 in 1871 dollars. It is a typical example of what was rotten and crooked in early day Nevada. Pioche had about 10,000 residents at the time. It now has a few hundred and the courthouse is now an interesting museum.

Minden and Gardnerville

Minden
Germany

Minden
Nevada

Twin cities in northern Nevada. Citizens of Minden, Germany settled the town. Immigrants from the Basque country of France settled in Gardnerville.

Mine Shafts

There are at least 10,000 mine shafts in Nevada, almost all of them abandoned. Whatever else you do out in the desert, do not enter any old mines. Once you slide down one of those shafts it is almost impossible to get back out. They have water in the bottom, and snakes, spiders and bats hide in them. They also cave in quite easily. So, stay away.

Minsky's Follies

At the Dunes Hotel in 1957 was the first topless show in Las Vegas.

Misfits Flat

Misfits Flats

Misfits Flat off Highway 50 near Stagecoach takes its name from the John Huston film. Huston used the privately owned area to film a complicated wild horse round up with Clark Gable, Marilyn Monroe, Montgomery Clift and Eli Wallach.

Mormon Wagon Trail

THE MORMON WAGON TRAIL

Was laid out following the Spanish Trail. It led from Salt Lake City to Las Vegas.

Mormon Battalion

Fanned out from Salt Lake City and had orders to secure parts of the West. They built a so-called "fort" in Las Vegas on North Las Vegas Boulevard near Cashman Field.

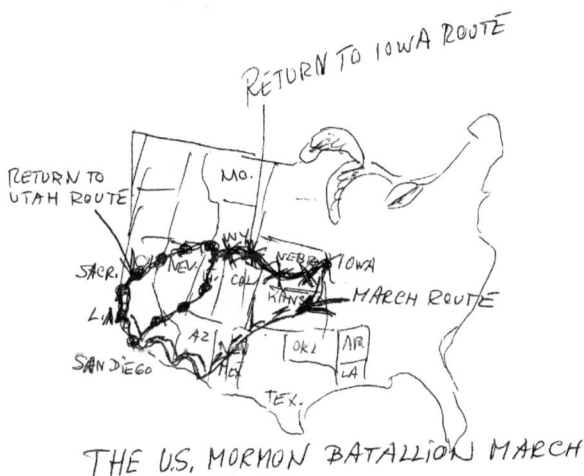

THE U.S. MORMON BATALLION MARCH

Moulin Rouge

Is on Lake Mead, close to D Street. In early Las Vegas, African-American performers could work on the Strip, but they could not stay there. Las Vegas was totally segregated. The "West Side" developed many black owned casinos, bars, shops, etc., places with names such as

Town Tavern, El Morocco Club, and Harlem Club. The Town Tavern was renamed the New Town Tavern and was the last club to survive. It is ironic that famous African-American performers like Sammy Davis Jr., Lena Horne, and Nat "King" Cole could work on the Strip but were not allowed to get a room there. Another strange thing: African-Americans originally did not live there, but around Stewart Street. They were pushed out of that area and into the West Side. One more thing, during monsoon times that area is one of the few that does not flood.

Mountains

Nevada has more mountain ranges than any other state, with its highest point at the 13,145 foot top of Boundary Peak near the west-central border. There are 315 mountain ranges.

Most Expensive Room/Suite

The Palms hotel has a suite for $25,000 per. That is a sweet deal as of this writing. It is only a matter of time before some other company wants to top that.

Most Expensive Burger

You can get it at the Burger Brasserie inside the Paris hotel for a mere $777. I usually buy two for lunch.

Most Expensive Pastry

It can be had (it is a cupcake) at the Palazzo for $750 per piece as of the writing of this book. Go ahead, order a half dozen.

Movies

To date about 116 movies were made that either mention Nevada, or were made in Nevada. Some notable ones are: Nevada Smith, The Ox Bow Incident, Fear and Loathing in Las Vegas, Oceans Eleven, Rainman, Vanishing Point, Breakdown, Lethal Weapon, and others.

Musical Fountains

The fountains at the Bellagio Hotel are choreographed to music. They cost $40 million to install.

Mustang Ranch

Storey County, a few miles up the road (east) from Reno. Allegedly the largest legal brothel in the U.S. Some entrepreneur some years ago wanted it listed on the stock exchange (the Pink Sheets maybe?) For years run by Joe Conforte who disappeared to Argentina because the Feds wanted him on tax evasion charges. I remember him as a very generous tipper whenever he came into my place of employment – usually with two or three of his extremely pretty ladies. A heavyweight boxer met his untimely demise on a barbed wire fence at that place. He was an Argentinian guy by the name of Oscar Bonaventura.

Naked City

Has also been called Silicon Valley. A run-down area north of Sahara Avenue and west of Las Vegas Boulevard. It was formerly home to many showgirls who had a propensity for nude sunbathing, hence the name.

Native Americans

There are three native American tribes in Nevada: the Washoe, Paiute and Shoshone

Natives

Nevada has the lowest percentage of native born residents. Only 1 out of every 5 Nevada residents were born in the state (as of 2014).

Neon, Neon, Neon

There are about 15,000 miles of neon tubing in Las Vegas.

Nevada Gambling Museum

It is in Virginia City at 22 South C Street.

Nevada, Lincoln and the Civil War

Nevada was granted Statehood during the Civil War. The State motto is "Battle Born." Lincoln needed the money generated by the mines to conduct the war.

Nevada State Prison

This is one of the oldest territorial prisons in the west. It has been closed since 2012. Efforts are being launched to reopen it as a museum. Several movies were made featuring the prison, including one starring Tom Selleck (1989 – An Innocent Man). The prison is located at the state capital, Carson City.

Nevada Test Site

100 miles North of Las Vegas, now officially called the Nevada National Security Site. This area is larger than some Eastern states. This is where they blow the big ones. When you see 1950's photos of tourists in Las Vegas casually watching nuclear mushroom clouds in the distance, this is that place. A crater caused by one test in 1962, the Sedan Crater, can be seen clearly on online aerial photos such as Google Earth. Far from being benign, the testing left high levels of radiation in the soil and groundwater, and caused increased cases of cancer in workers at the site as well as civilians living downwind in Utah. In recent years there has been an ongoing battle over using the site to store nuclear waste created out-of-state.

The site can be visited via a monthly tour which leaves Las Vegas at 7:30 a.m. and returns around 4 p.m. Strict security prevails. U.S. Citizens need to make reservations three weeks in advance. Then bring photo ID with Social Security number on it. Non-citizens need to make reservations 6 weeks in advance. I cannot rate that place, I have never been there. I can't imagine they let you see a lot. The Russians probably know more about it than we do.

Newlands

This project is located in Fallon, southeast of Reno, and was the first Federal attempt to irrigate desert areas for crop production. The Lahontan Dam was built around 1911 to divert water from the Carson River. A famous crop widely available in northern Nevada during harvest time is the "Hearts of Gold" cantaloupe, an especially sweet and juicy variety. This project accomplished two things: it irrigated land and it shafted the local Native Americans at Pyramid Lake by depriving them of their water. They had their homes at the edge of the lake. Now they live inland. The strange part is, at that time the U.S. really did not need any more agricultural products.

Nick Civella

March 3, 1912–March 12, 1983. Was a mob enforcer in Las Vegas. He managed to become one of the first entries into the Nevada "black book." The book contains the names of people who have run afoul of Nevada law and are denied access to casinos statewide.

No One Home

Esmeralda County is one of the least populated counties in the lower 48. Each person, in fact, has three square miles available. Only Loving County in Texas has less people per square mile. It is ironic, because the county seat, Goldfield; was once the largest city west of Chicago with an estimated population of 30,000.

Odds

The best odds of any casino game can be found at the craps table. That is as long as you don't play the field and the proposition bets, the hard eight or hard six. And if you do not take full odds on all your bets I will personally come over and kick your butt. By playing the game right you can shave the casino advantage down to a fraction of a percent. All you need then is a tiny bit of luck.

Oldest Bank Building

The oldest bank building is in Austin. The bank was in business from 1863 – 1962.

Oldest Human Mummy

The oldest human mummy in North America was found in 1940 in Spirit Cave by husband and wife archeologists Sydney and Georgia Wheeler. The cave is 17 miles east of Fallon.

Neon Boneyard

This is soooo Las Vegas. A collection of discarded neon signs. Most of them are off strip hotels, but there are also unique signs from other businesses that have fortunately been saved, like the old Chief Motel, formerly on Fremont Street. They even shipped the lobby of the old La Concha motel over there. Pretty neat!

New York New York

Is the only casino on the Strip without its own marquee. They recently added some lettering on an addition they built alongside the strip.

Oldest Newspaper

The oldest continuously published newspaper in Nevada is the Reese River Reveille, in Austin, which started in 1863 and is still being published.

Oldest Residence

The oldest permanent European-American residence seems to be the Virgin River Mormon residence that was built in 1840. It still stands and is still occupied.

Old Mormon Fort

The Old Mormon Fort Is located off Las Vegas Boulevard North, close to Cashman Field. It is quite a stretch to call this a fort. It is a small, unassuming adobe building.

OLD MORMON FORT LAS VEGAS, NV

Old Spanish Trail

This is the old trail between Santa Fe, New Mexico and Los Angeles, California. Keep in mind that all that area was controlled by Mexico at the time. At first it was a horse trail but later the 49ers used it as a wagon trail to California. Mormon pioneers also used this trail. About 130 miles of the Spanish Trail are in Clark County and run roughly between Mesquite, Town Center, Blue Diamond, Mountain Springs and Fantasy Park in Las Vegas.

Old Spanish Trail at Mountain Springs Pass

A very popular spot on the Old Spanish Trail for a stopover. It is much cooler in the summer, with springs and meadows. It took two days from here to Las Vegas and a stopover was required at Cottonwood Springs. That stopover is now called Blue Diamond.

Old Spanish Trail - Garces Expedition

Francisco Garces was a Franciscan priest who used Indian guides to travel from the Colorado River to San Gabriel, California in March of 1776. He followed a very old Indian trail.

Old Spanish Trail - Armijo's Route

THE OLD SPANISH TRAIL
Dominguez - Escalante Expedition

Antonio Armijo was a merchant who led the first successful pack train across the Las Vegas Valley in 1830. He traveled all the way from Santa Fe, New Mexico to Los Angeles, California thereby opening a new trade route. An almost unbelievable feat in those days covering over a thousand miles and through hostile, bandit ridden areas. In those days New Mexico, California and everything in between belonged to Mexico. A member of Armijos group, Raphael Rivera, is generally credited with the discovery of the Las Vegas valley.

Old Spanish Trail - The Journey of Death

It is the 55 mile stretch of the trail between the Muddy River and Las Vegas. The Spanish called it "journada del muerto." There was no water and most traders traveled at night. The first fresh water after leaving the Muddy River was in Las Vegas itself. It is the longest waterless stretch on the Spanish Trail. Actually very similar to the trail leading into Reno from the Humboldt Sink (Forty Mile Desert).

One Million Dollars

Is on display at Binion's Hotel/Casino in downtown Las Vegas. You can have your picture taken in front of it. It is all encased in a solid block of plastic.

Opal

The state gemstone is black fire opal, a rare and beautiful stone that is found in large quantities only in Nevada.

Overland Trail

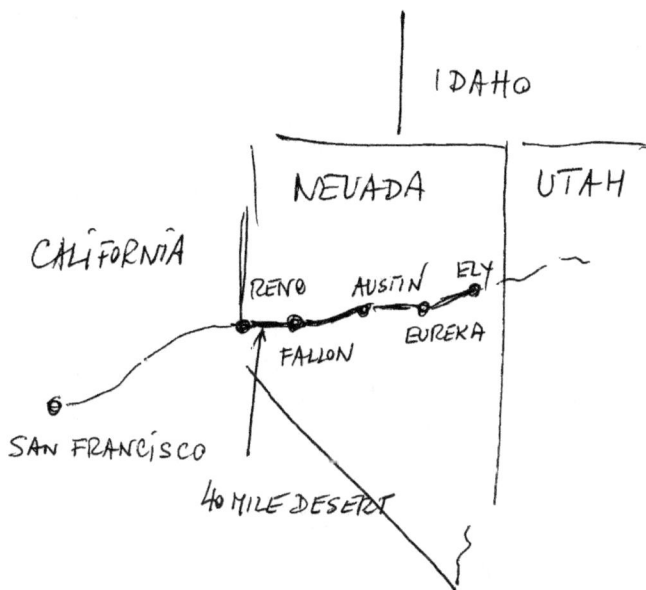

THE OVERLAND TRAIL
THROUGH NEVADA

The Overland Trail (also known as the Overland Stage Line) was a stagecoach and wagon trail in the American West during the 19th century. While portions of the route had been used by explorers and trappers since the 1820's, the Overland Trail was most heavily used in the 1860's as an alternative route to the Oregon, California and Mormon trails through central Wyoming. The Overland Trail was famously used by the Overland Stage Company owned by Ben Holladay to run mail and passengers to Salt Lake City, Utah, via stagecoaches in the early 1860's. Starting from Atchison, Kansas, the trail descended into Colorado before looping back up to southern Wyoming and rejoining the Oregon Trail at Fort Bridger. The stage line operated until 1869 when the completion of the First Transcontinental Railroad eliminated the need for mail service via stagecoach.

Panaca

Is a variation of the Southern Paiute word pa-na-ka meaning metal. The town of Panaca tried to secede from Nevada in 1864, because of lower land taxes in Utah.

Performing Elephant

Bertha performed at John Ascuaga's Nugget in Sparks for 37 years. She died at age 48.

Pick Handle Gulch

This miniscule, out of the way and unlikely town was the birth place of one James E. Casey. James went on to greatness when he founded, with his brothers, UPS, United Parcel Service. He became a member of the U.S. Department of Labor Hall of Fame. Pick Handle Gulch was later renamed Metallic City.

Pilot Peak

Can be seen almost a hundred miles away in Tooele, Utah. Emigrants used it for navigation.

Pioche

Named after a San Francisco financier. The town was notorious for the numerous gunfights that took place. A large portion, well over 50% of all murders in the state took place there. All in all about $50 million of silver came out of those mines.

Pony Express

Only operated for less than two years. Sacramento was the Western Terminus. Carson City, south of Reno, was one of their relay stations.

Across Nevada about 30 relay stations were installed. Quite a feat of organizing.. Their riders meals consisted of beans, bread and beef. They could have whiskey, but had to pay for it. The meal was free. The riders only carried a mochila (mail bag), a pistol, beef jerky, horn and bible. They relied on the superior speed of their horse and avoided fights. Only one rider was killed in eighteen months of hard riding.

Pony Express - Butte Valley Station

This was the most feared stop by pony express riders of the entire Pony Express route. It lies thirty miles west of Cherry Creek in White Pine County. It had no shade, very little water and was under constant Indian attack. Most riders rode directly on to Diamond Springs, another fifty miles to the west. That is a tremendous distance by horse.

PONY EXPRESS STATION
WHITE PINE COUNTY

Pony Express - White Pine County Station

Not much left, just some rocks. Interesting nevertheless.

Pony Express - Ruby Valley Station

Built in 1860, closed in 1861. Moved to Elko in 1960 and is now part of a museum exhibit in that city. It is one of only two surviving stations.

RUBY VALLEY

Pony Express - Cold Springs Station

COLD SPRINGS

It is on U.S. 50, 56 miles west of Austin, in Churchill County.

Pony Express - Diamond Springs Station

Located near the mouth of Telegraph Canyon. It is named after Jack Diamond, a miner and prospector. The exact location is N 39.54.47.7 and W 115-52-21.2 in Eureka County. Don't look for buildings, not much is left.

Potosi

This was an important lead mine for the Mormon miners who discovered it. They called it "the mountain of lead." It was also an important source of zinc during World War I. What is interesting is the fact there are several Potosi mines around the world. One in Spain, another in Bolivia. That one is called "Cero Rico" is a silver mine, and has been continuously mined for three hundred years.

Praying Mantis

At the entrance of the Container Park in Las Vegas, on East Fremont street, a giant praying mantis scares little kids. It's a modified military vehicle reaching several stories tall, and emits fire and smoke at certain times.

Prostitution

It is legal in Nevada, it is a county option. So you have two counties without it. They are Washoe and Clark, essentially Reno and Las Vegas. If you feel like having a little action go to the Mustang Ranch, the Chicken Ranch, Mabel's Ranch or the Green Door.

Rabbit Hole

Northern Nevada around Winnemucca. Large gold bearing area with microscopic gold. One of the largest gold mines in the world located nearby.

Ragtown x 2

After crossing the 40 mile desert the emigrants (those that were left) would clean up and do their washing and hang it in the breeze. It is near Fallon, some miles east of Reno.

RAG TOWN

There was another Rag Town near Lake Mead. Men and women, desperate for work during the height of the depression, gathered around Lake Mead where they erected a town built out of scrap lumber and rags. They could not enter Boulder City proper or the dam site because armed guards had been stationed there. Conditions at the site can best be described as hellish. Temperatures in that area can go up to 120° F. No air conditioning existed at the time. The drawing is from a contemporary photograph.

Railroads

Nevada is full of ghost towns and abandoned railroads. At least fifty lines were in operation at one time or the other. The most famous was the short haul Virginia City and Truckee Line, sometimes called the "richest railroad in the world." It hauled ore and equipment from the Comstock Lode. But there are other gems, a lot of them very short lived. One line ran from Elko to a copper smelter in Ely. That also is the location of one of the largest "glory holes" in the U.S. It is an open pit copper mine, now defunct.

Railroad Tunnels

There are five of them on the trail above Lake Mead to Hoover Dam. The trail was the old railroad bed that ran to the dam construction site in the 1930's. The trail head is below the visitors' center. The end of the trail is the top floor of the parking garage at Hoover Dam. It's accessible for both hiking and biking. To get there take the I-93 from Boulder City, turn off at the Lake Mead Visitor Center turn-off. Drive about one mile and you will spot the parking lot on the right. From there just follow the signs. Parking is free, so is the hiking.

Rainbow Curve

On Route 95 in Las Vegas where it turns south at Rainbow Boulevard.

Ranching in Nevada

Is not at all like ranching in Pennsylvania or Michigan. Some parts of the state require 35 (that's right, thirty-five) acres of land to raise a head of cattle. On top of this cattle have to be shipped out of state for finishing off in feed lots. Round-ups are conducted by motorcycle, jeep and even helicopter. The Petan Ranch reportedly has 250,000 acres. There also used to be a Bonanza (remember the TV show?)

Raphael Rivera

He was an early day scout who blazed a route from the Amargosa River to the Mojave River in California. This became a vital link of the Old Spanish Trail. It was known in this area as the Mormon Trail. When the Antonio Armijo trading group camped about 60 miles away from the Las Vegas valley in 1829, Raphael struck out on his own and stumbled upon the Las Vegas valley. He was the first non-native to set foot in the area.

Rawhide
Central Nevada

Once a thriving town, now totally deserted. Like many another town in the old west, this one was destroyed by fire. Was the home of Tex Rickard's "Northern Saloon," a boxing promoter who staged the Nelson/Gans fight in Goldfield. That fight was stopped after 42 (yes, forty-two) rounds because of an illegal punch or butt, a "foul." Remember we are talking bare knuckle fighting here. I actually once rented a room in Reno from a very old lady who once was a teacher in Rawhide.

TEX RICKARD

Real Estate and Water

Do not buy land in Nevada unless you know you have water and/or water rights. Consult a lawyer!!

Reno

Reno is named after Major General Jesse Lee Reno, U.S. Army who was killed in a Civil War battle on September 14, 1862 in Boonsboro, Frederick County, Maryland.

Reno's Chinatown

In the late 1800's Reno began to experience a series of smallpox, cholera and other infectious diseases. Vaccines were unknown at the time. The source was traced to an area of town inhabited by Chinese immigrants. The inhabitants were relocated and several square blocks were burned down on orders of the city council. Soon thereafter the diseases stopped occurring.

Republic of Molossia

In Dayton, south of Reno. It is a guy with a uniform, a shack and a small piece of land. The president, king, prime minister? is Kevin Baugh. It originally was the Grand Republic of Vuldstein and encompasses a total of 6.4 acres. In 2006 armed conflict broke out with Musachistan and its leader Sultan Ali-Ali Ochsenfree. The Valora is the official currency. T-shirts are available in all sizes.

Ringbolts

During the early days of steamboat navigation on the Colorado the boats could not make it through the rapids without help. So, they used ringbolts (eye-bolts) to pull themselves through. If you want to see them you need to go to "Ringbolt Rapids" below Hoover Dam, where a few of the ring bolts are still in place. I have seen a good example of a ringbolt at Willow Beach on the east side of the Colorado River not too far from Boulder City.

River Crossings

Only two towns in Nevada were founded because they were at a river crossing. Reno (original name Lake's Crossing) and Wellington. It is vastly different from other states.

Roller Coasters

The roller coaster at the NewYork NewYork hotel runs right through the casino. The roller coaster at Primm does the same thing.

Ronald Reagan in Las Vegas

R.R. made his only night club appearance in Las Vegas.

Roulette

Add up all numbers on a roulette table and you wind up with 666

Round Courthouse

Pershing County has the only round court house in the U.S.A.

Rhyolite

RHYOLITE

Ghost town about 80 miles from Las Vegas.. Once one of the largest cities in these parts with about 10,000 people, 50 saloons and 18 grocery stores. Even had its own railroad. The old depot is still standing, also part of the bank building. Most of the rest of the town has blown away. Can also be reached via Beatty. A huge gold mine is nearby, practically at the doorsteps. See, there is still gold in them thar hills.

Roads

Movie producers seem to like Nevada roads. They have been featured in a variety of films such as Vanishing Point, Breakdown, Rainman, Lethal Weapon and others.

Rooms

Las Vegas has more hotel rooms than any other place on earth. It would take almost 300 years for a person to sleep one night in each hotel room in Las Vegas. And more are coming!

St. Valentines Day Massacre

The wall in front of which the gangsters were killed is in the Mob Museum in Las Vegas.

Sand Mountain

Remains of an ancient lake near Fallon.

Saved by Nudity

When the Dunes Hotel opened quite a bit south of other large hotels on the strip it could not attract enough customers to stay afloat. In a stroke of genius the first topless show, "Minsky's Follies," was booked into the showroom. Almost immediately things turned around and the hotel started to make money, enough money in fact to start on expansion and to add a golf course. Some years later the Dunes was also the first hotel with a gigantic, electric advertising sign. The Dunes was imploded and the Bellagio took its place.

Sarah Winnemucca

The first Native American woman to write a history of her tribe and her autobiography in 1883. Rather remarkable.

Scary Rides

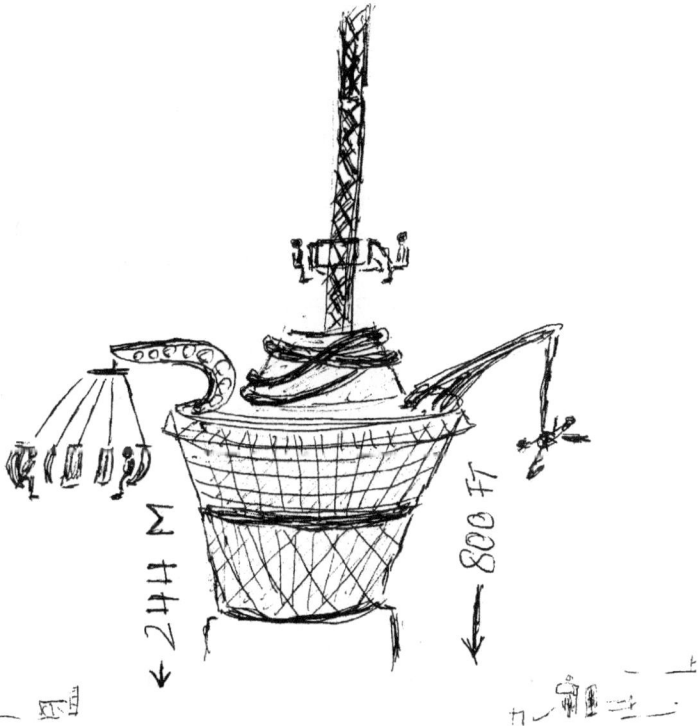

The Stratosphere in Las Vegas is the tallest free-standing, observation tower in the US and the tallest structure west of the Mississippi River. The top of the Stratosphere has three very scary, but popular, rides. They shoot you into space, let you hang outside the building 800 feet above the ground, and fling you in circles.

Sculptures

For outdoor sculptures the place to go to is Boulder City. They have them on about every downtown street corner. Big ones, small ones, bronze, clay and everything in between. Really interesting stuff.

Searchlight

A town not unlike many other small western towns, but yet very remarkable in some ways. Gold ore was discovered here in 1897 and the town soon had rail service. In 1923 the track was washed out and service was never restored. It is remarkable because Harry Reid, the only Senate Majority leader from Nevada, was born and raised in this small town. He can still periodically be seen having breakfast in a small casino cafe. Story has it that a certain Mr. Colton, who founded the town, said "There's gold in them thar hills, but you need a searchlight to find it." It also was a brand of matches.

Sedan Crater

This crater is the largest man made crater in the western hemisphere. It was created during Project Plowshare, a series of underground atomic tests. For this test a 105 kiloton atomic charge was set off about 600 feet underground. As it turned out the charge was not buried deep enough. It created a crater 300 feet deep and 1,300 feet across. The resulting fall out affected 13 million people and effectively ended the program. The blast happened on July 6, 1962. About 6.6 million tons of earth was displaced. The crater is at Area 1, Yucca Flats and can be visited with prior appointment.

Self Parking

Sure, you can self park your car or truck almost anywhere in this state. But some very special areas have flying saucer self parking.

Settlements

Nevada has a little more than 100 towns. Out of all those less than 30 have more than 1,000 inhabitants.

Shark Tank Water Slide

The Golden Nugget Hotel on Fremont Street in downtown Las Vegas has a water slide that takes people through a tank with live sharks.

Shoe Tree

Churchill, on Highway 51, the loneliest road in America.

Shoes

It is against the law to use x-rays for selling shoes.

Short Lived Rail Road

The Silver Peak Rail Road was built in 1883 and lived for an astounding ten months.

Shrimp

More of this delicacy is consumed per day in Las Vegas than in the rest of the country combined: 60,000 pounds.

Silicon Valley

A topless club. Specifically the Olympic Gardens topless club.

Silver Queen

It is a fifteen foot high painting of a lady at the Silver Queen bar in Virginia City. Her dress is made of 3,200 silver dollars

Slot Machines

There are now 13,000 fewer slot machines on the Las Vegas Strip than at the beginning of the 2008 recession. By 2013 the number was about 45,000. Keep in mind that a lot of slot machines now feature multiple games. Still, the recession took its toll.

By state law slot machines are supposed to pay out at least 75% of the money gambled. How is that for odds? They guarantee you will lose 25% of every dollar played.

Slot Addiction

Gamblers who play the slot machines on a regular basis will become addicted to them within a year according to a study by Robert Breen, psychiatrist at Brown University. I have personal knowledge of several of my friends sinking into abject poverty because of slot/gambling addiction.

Some friendly and some not so friendly desert dwellers

Snakes, Scorpions, Black Widows, Gila Monsters, Tarantulas, Killer Bees, Fire Ants and Brown Recluse Spiders

DESERT SURVIVORS

Stay away from that spider! It inflicts a nasty bite that makes the flesh around the wound rot. Two snakes in Nevada, the Western Rattler and the Sidewinder, are both very poisonous. The rattler has an extremely fast strike and injects an enormous amount of venom. Get thee to a doctor fast or prepare thee to meet thy maker. Fortunately, rattlers only move at a certain temperature. When it is really hot or cold you have nothing to fear. They also try to stay away from humans. There is supposed to be a Coral Snake in the Sierra Nevada. I have never seen one. The Gila Monster is a colorful salamander that really needs to be provoked before it will do anything. You nearly have to put your finger in its mouth. They are also very rare. Tarantulas are really quite harmless and rarely seen in these parts. I have only seen one in twenty five years. Scorpions are nasty little buggers with a bad sting. They are a new import to the Las Vegas Valley. They are real good climbers and have no trouble entering your living quarters. They show up at night under UV light and are easy to find that way. Black Widows are really pitch black and have a red hourglass on their bellies. They are pretty poisonous but not lethal (in most cases). Killer Bees have made their way to Southern Nevada. They are very aggressive and attack en masse. Keep your eyes open. Fire ants are another recent arrival. Stay away from them too!

Smallest Casino on the Strip

That honor goes to the Slots-A-Fun, next to the CircusCircus. That company bought it some years ago, but it is a separate building with its own logo.

Snowshoe Thompson

A Norwegian immigrant Thompson (or Thomson) was said to be the only person at that time able to cross the Sierra Nevada mountain range in the dead of winter, carrying the U.S. Mail. He made his first trip in 1856. His average trip time was three days carrying a pack of 80 pounds and more, truly amazing. Keep in mind these mountains receive 30-40 feet of snow per season. He did it on skis he made, which were allegedly about ten feet in length. He was no overnight wonder: he made the trip for twenty years by himself. He also owned a small ranch in the vicinity. In the end the U.S. Postal Service managed to cheat him out of his pay. He delivered the mail anyway. Thompson is buried in the little town of Genoa in northern Nevada. Genoa itself was formerly a stop on the Overland Express stagecoach route. Now very small, it is famous for its annual "Candy Dance." Thompson's feats were described by reporter Dan DeQuille, a reporter for the Territorial Enterprise which was started in Genoa but later moved to Virginia City. Another well known scribe for that publication was none other than Mark Twain.

Some Silly Laws

From around the State.

It is illegal to drive a camel on a Nevada highway.

In Eureka it is illegal for a man wearing a mustache to kiss a woman.

In Nevada it is legal to hang a person for shooting your dog on your property.

In Elko you must wear a mask while walking in the street.

In Las Vegas it is illegal to pawn your dentures.

In Las Vegas you may bet on any sports team in the country, but not on UNLV.

In Reno it is illegal to stage a dance marathon. You may promote one by hanging a notice about it on a fire hydrant.

In Reno it is (or was) illegal to have a brothel within 400 yards of a school or church.

More about Reno: It is illegal to hide a spray painted shopping cart in your basement.

It is against the law in Reno to place a bench in the middle of the street.

In Reno, sex toys are illegal.

In Reno it is illegal to lie down on the sidewalk.

Space

Nevada has more open space than any other place in the lower 48 states. Over 80% of Nevada's land is designated for public and recreational use.

Spaghetti Bowl

The interchange of I-95 and I-15 in downtown Las Vegas.

Sparks and Wadsworth

Sparks was once the largest Union Pacific depot/machine shop/repair shop/turntable in Nevada. When the workers started a strike, the U.P. superintendent simply gave orders to move all equipment, shops, turntables, and rails to a different location, Wadsworth, to be precise. End of strike. On top of it all the guy got to name his own town. Can you guess his name?

Sphinx

The Sphinx at the entrance of the Luxor hotel is, at 101 feet larger than the original.

Sports Books

The old Stardust was the first hotel to install a sports book. The idea came from none other than Frank (Lefty) Rosenthal.

Stateline

Anywhere in Nevada where gaming clubs have been built close to a state line in order to take advantage of incoming traffic from the adjoining state. For instance, Primm on I-15 from California to Nevada, or Jackpot, catching traffic from Idaho to Nevada. The most famous one is on the North Shore of Lake Tahoe where the state line runs through the center of the casino of the Nevada Lodge.

Statue of Liberty

There are two of them in Las Vegas. A large one is at the New York New York Hotel. Another can be found at a small strip mall at 4211 West Sahara Avenue. It was built in 1981, is forty feet tall, and the base at one time was a pizza drive-thru.

Strange Roads

U.S. 6 and U.S. 50 are the same highway from Ely, Nevada to Delta, Utah, some 155 miles. It is the third longest stretch of road in the U.S. to have two highway numbers designated to it. Speaking of Ely, that town seems to attract strange roads. It is one of only three places in the U.S. where three U.S. routes converge: U.S. 6, U.S. 50 and U.S. 93.

St. Thomas

This town was abandoned when the rising waters of Lake Mead reached it. Its ruins can be seen from time to time during periods of drought when the lake experiences low water. It is in Nevada at the north shore of Lake Mead.

Stokes Castle

It is located close to the now almost deserted town of Austin. Austin was a prominent silver camp that flourished around the 1860's. There are still a few hundred residents hanging on. The castle itself is more like a square rock tower and was built by A.P. Stokes, a mining and railroad baron. Built as a replica of a tower outside of Rome, Italy, the tower was occupied only once by Stokes and his family. After that the "castle" was abandoned. One of the stranger stories in the state. The first floor has the kitchen and dining room, the second floor the living room and the third floor two bedrooms. The roof had an outside living room with curtains to keep out the dust.

Strange Directions

To drive from Los Angeles, California to Reno, Nevada the direction traveled is to the west.

Street Names

When it comes to street names, anything goes in Las Vegas. Well, almost anything. Nothing is too strange or outlandish. There are a few streets named after alcoholic beverages. Then there are those streets that are named after casinos, such as Tropicana, Flamingo, Sahara, and Desert Inn. Those actually make a lot of sense. You have streets named after fruits, nuts, art, magic, entertainment other countries, other cities. The list goes on and on. There are even streets named after The Hobbit and the Beatles. (Middle Earth Street, Yesterday Drive). Gomer and Pyle are parallel streets. Get yourself Google Maps and see what other odd names you can find. I assure you, there are plenty.

Stupid Bets

A group of workers got caught in 1980 betting on when the patient would die at the hospital that employed them.

Surviving the Desert

How much water is enough? Experts recommend a gallon of water per day when out in the desert in the summer. So, using this information and knowing how much water weighs (8.34 pounds per gallon) we can interpolate how much we can carry. It isn't much, not enough to survive on for maybe a few days. In other words, "stay out of the desert and stay on main roads."

Sutro

Adolph Heinrich Joseph Sutro arrived in California from Germany in 1850. A mining engineer by trade, he stayed in San Francisco for a while, engaging in business. He moved to Nevada and got interested again in mining. After hearing of water and ventilation problems in the mines he devised a plan to drain the mines by drilling a tunnel through the mountain. He moved back to California and became very wealthy. He died on August 8, 1898.

Taxes

Nevada is one of only nine states without an income tax.

Temple of Sekhmet

This is located near Indian Springs—yes, the same Indian Springs that is famous for being near Area 51. It was built around 1995 by a bunch of peaceniks. The name refers to an ancient Egyptian goddess with the head of a lion. It is still open to the public and exists mainly on donations and a gift shop. You can actually stay overnight, provided you make arrangements in advance. There also is a sweat lodge. Not that you really need one here in the summer. Call them at 702-596-0630 if you want to do that spiritual thing. They are about 50 miles north of the Las Vegas Strip.

Tennis

Andre Agassi and his wife Steffi Graf are famous tennis stars who make their home in Las Vegas. They are both very engaged in charitable work and many of the buildings they created for that purpose are located in minority areas, for instance the Agassi Academy.

The Lakes

A large credit card company wanted to build a service center in Las Vegas. They did not want their "good" name to be associated with Las Vegas. Solution: just name it The Lakes and get a separate zip code. It is on West Sahara Avenue.

The Secessionist Movement

In 1867 the Nevada Legislature voted to include present day Clark County, which includes Las Vegas, into the state. Up until that time it was part of Arizona Territory. They forgot one important thing: they forgot to amend the Nevada Constitution to reflect the new boundaries. So, in the 1980's Nevada voters had to shuffle to the voting booth and vote on it. At that time there were a sizable number of people that wanted Clark County to secede from the state.

Thunder Mountain Monument

THUNDER MOUNTAIN

Huge monument built by an artist who called himself Chief Rolling Thunder. It is in Imlay.

124

Tobar

TO BAR

It was the direction sign for a bar. That is so Nevada, naming a whole town after a saloon. The real meaning was "to the bar", or "this way to the bar". Of the town only a few sticks and stones are left way out there in the desert.

Toilet Paper Man

Nothing is too outlandish for Nevada. In Boulder City you can admire the statue of the toilet paper man. He was a worker at the dam when it was under construction. They called him Alabam, it was his job to make sure all toilets had adequate supplies of toilet paper.

Tonopah

Also called "The Queen of the Silver Camps," it was the second largest silver strike, right behind Virginia City. This semi-ghost town is a fair way from Las Vegas, going north on Route 95, midway to Reno. I mention it here because of Wyatt Earp who was the sheriff and Jack

WYATT EARP

JACK DEMPSEY

Dempsey, the boxer, who once lived there. Dempsey was actually a bartender/bouncer in one of the saloons. The town sits at a very high elevation, 6,047 feet (1,843 meters). Try and get there during their Jim Butler Days in May. They have mucking contests, gold panning, arm wresting, a parade and more. The actual vein of silver ore was allegedly found by someone's donkey. Another strange fact: the ore that was mined was first hauled by horse and wagon to the nearby town of Austin and then shipped to Salt Lake for smelting. All in all, about five million tons of ore have been produced in Tonopah. In 1903 riots broke out in protest against Chinese immigrant miners. Those riots prompted the Chinese government to boycott U.S. goods.

Topless Shows

The Dunes, demolished in 1993, was the first resort to feature topless showgirls in a show called Minsky's Follies.

A Famous Train Robber

On November 4, 1870, Andrew Jackson Davis, "Big Jack" and his gang robbed the Central Pacific Rail Road between Reno and Verdi of $40,000 in gold and silver coins. The cops were able to track them down and arrest the gang. Big Jack did time in the Nevada State Prison and was let out on good behavior. Soon after he got out he robbed a stage coach and he was shot and killed on September 3, 1877. The story does not end here. There are rumors the train robbers had time to hide some of their train robbery loot between Reno and Verdi. People have been looking for it for the last hundred years and more.

Trading Routes

The years 1831-1832 saw the beginning of Mexican trading caravans from Santa Fe, New Mexico to Los Angeles, California. An enormous distance in those days.

Tule Springs

If you are interested in ancient fossils, then this is for you. This place is almost in downtown Las Vegas, so to speak, being only 25 miles north of the Strip. Here you can dig for the Giant Mammoth, the Giant Ground Sloth, the Sabre Tooth Cat, American Lion and Dire Wolf. You need to hurry though. Developers have their eye on this piece of property. Tule (pronounced too-lee) is a giant rush that grows in marshes.

Tunnel of Love

It is a drive through wedding chapel at 130 South Las Vegas Boulevard. It takes an entire 15 minutes and costs $40 to get hitched.

Unincorporated Town #1

For three years that was the name of the town we now know as Jackpot. It sits along the Idaho-Nevada line. Originally just a trailer town, in fact for years there was no conventional building, just trailers.

Union Pacific and Central Pacific Railroad

One of the great engineering feats in the Old West. Traverses the Sierra Nevada from Reno to Auburn through numerous tunnels. Some of the track actually runs under roofs (officially they are called sheds) because of the heavy snowfall in those mountains.

Uranium King

Charles E. Steen was a down on his luck miner when, on July 6, 1952 he hit it big and made a huge fortune with the discovery of a massive deposit of uranium ore at Big Indian Wash of Lisbon Valley, southeast of Moab, Utah. A huge number of prospectors and miners rushed to the area, similar to the California gold rush. He later moved his family to Washoe Valley, south of Reno, not far from the other mining magnate Bowers. Steen lost all his money by poor investments and tax liens. He declared bankruptcy in 1968 and died Jan. 1, 2006 in Colorado.

Utah and Nevada

Nevada used to be part of Utah Territory, an enormous piece of land. On March 2, 1861, President Buchanan signed an Act of Congress making Nevada a Territory. It included all of present day Nevada, except the area of Clark County, which was ceded to Nevada from Arizona in 1866.

Vegas Vic and Vegas Vicky

Vegas Vic is a 40-foot tall, neon-outlined cowboy figure who stands above the former Pioneer Club on Fremont Street. He was erected in 1951 and used to wave his hand, blow smoke rings and say "Howdy, pardner!" but he is along in years now and doesn't do much of anything. In 1980 they gave him a girlfriend across the street, the cowgirl Vegas Vicky. Vic is so tall that, when they built the canopy over Fremont Street, they had to modify both Vic and the canopy so he would fit under it. Vic and Vicky were married when the canopy was constructed in 1994. It is unknown which Vegas wedding chapel they patronized.

Venetian Hotel/Casino

The only hotel in the U.S. with an indoor canal and singing gondoliers.

The Venetian in Macao has three canals with singing gondoliers.

Very Short Rivers

The Truckee, the Carson and the Walker are all rivers of less than 125 miles in length. The Truckee originates in Lake Tahoe and disappears into Pyramid Lake. The other two rivers do similar tricks. They are the very few rivers running east from the Sierra Nevada rather than west.

Virginia City and the Comstock Lode

Once one of the richest silver deposits in the world. The town is still there, hanging on by a thread.

Virginia City and Truckee Railroad

Virginia & Truckee Train on the big trestle
"**INYO**"

At one time the richest short haul railroad in the US.

Visitors

80% of all visitors to Las Vegas are return visitors and average two trips per year. 44% of all visitors to Las Vegas arrive by air and 43% arrive by car. 89% of all visitors to Las Vegas gamble with an average gambling budget of $500. Over 38.9 million people visit Las Vegas each year (as of 2014).

State Boundary Monument

This is the boundary marker between California and Nevada. It can be found near Needles. It is an iron marker and was placed there in 1873 by Alexey W. Von Schmidt who was a surveyor and astronomer.

Walter Van Tilburgh Clark

Wrote several famous books: "City of Trembling Leaves" (refers to Reno, Nevada) and "The Ox Bow Incident," which was made into a movie starring Henry Fonda, Dana Andrews and Mary Beth Hughes. Also in the picture were Anthony Quinn and Harry Morgan.

Washoe County

The name derives from the Native American word "waashiw" meaning "the people from here." Source: Ancient Languages.

Wasteland

That's what a lot of people think of Nevada. Nothing but a big pile of rocks, sand and brush. But there is much more to it than just that. Crystal clear skies, no flies or mosquitoes to speak of. Endless vistas, ghost towns (about 10,000), scattered ranches, small settlements. In short, the desert has a certain charm that is different from other landscapes.

Water Babies

They are legendary demonic ghosts of babies that reside in Lake Tahoe and Pyramid Lake. According to an Indian legend they bring bad luck. According to urban legend, they devour fishermen who are never seen again.

Wayne Newton

WAYNE NEWTON

Started performing in Las Vegas at age 16. He holds the record for most performances in Las Vegas.

Weddings

Approximately 150 couples get married in Las Vegas each day.

Weeds Height

The same story as with Carp. It is named after a person, Clyde Weed, a mining C.E.O.

Wells

Started out in 1869 as a boxcar sitting along a railroad siding. It was used to sell rail tickets and to ship freight.

Wells Fargo

In 1861, if you wanted to travel east from California you had to first take the Pioneer stage to Carson City, Nevada. From there you took the Overland Mail Company stage to Salt Lake City for connections to the east. At first there was a southern route also, not through Nevada at all. It was the Butterfield Express Stage line through Texas and Indian territory. When that line shut down during the Civil War, folks had to take the Wells Fargo line. The Overland Mail Company had been bought by Wells Fargo. The stages traveled day and night with few rest stops, just long enough for fresh horses and coffee and some beef jerky.

Where is Pyramid?

This may sound odd, but the town of Pyramid is in Virginia City. When silver was discovered in Virginia City the good folks in Pyramid packed up the entire town and moved it to the new location. Pyramid was formerly located on the paved road leading from Reno to Pyramid Lake. Some foundation stones are still there. Watch out for the old time miner up on the hill a ways (if he is still there). He is gun crazy. He ran me off. I think he is mining copper up there by himself.

Who is in charge of the Strip?

The County Commissioners, that's who. The Strip is not in Las Vegas at all. It is in unincorporated Clark County.

Who is looking after all those sheep?

Mostly Basque sheepherders. They get special work permits. It is lonesome and dirty work. Out there, in the desert, all alone, just you and the sheep. I tried to talk to some of them but they all spoke French only. There are quite a few Basque restaurants in the northern part of the state, especially around Reno and Elko. Mostly family style dining.

Who owns Nevada?

The Feds, that's who, 85% of it.

Why is it so windy in Las Vegas?

In the spring and fall, high pressure builds in the Four Corners region, and air rushes in to fill the vacuum. In the fall the process is reversed.

Widow Maker

Also called miner's cough or silicosis. In the mining camp of Delamar alone no fewer than 1,000 miners died of it. In the Comstock a miner lasted until about age forty, then he died miserably, unable to breathe.

Winnemucca

The city is named after an Indian Chief. His name was Wobitsowahka, meaning "giver of spiritual gifts." It is the only incorporated city in Humboldt County, and with 201 sunny days it is also the sunniest city in Nevada.

Wyatt Earp

Enforced law and order for a while in Tonopah.

Wynn Hotel/Casino

The only hotel that has an indoor Ferrari dealership. When the hotel opened it was the most expensive in Las Vegas.

Yerington

Named after the former president of the Carson and Colorado Railroad.

You are in Paradise

Yes you are. The Strip is not in Las Vegas proper. It is in Clark County, in Paradise Township

Yucca Mountain Repository

A large tunnel built to hold atomic waste for the next 10,000 years. The Feds have spent billions to have it built and then shut it down. It is in Area 51 but only about 100 miles from Las Vegas.

24 Hour Television

Yes, my children. At one time, not too long ago, TV stations would actually sign-off at midnight or 1 a.m. When Howard Hughes came to Las Vegas he wanted to be able to watch TV at any time during the day or night. But there was nothing available. Solution: buy the station. Channel 5 is still around, H.H. is not.

Zip Lines

There are some amazing zip lines around Nevada. Here are two of the best: Fremont Street in downtown Las Vegas. Zip right in between a bunch of casinos and over throngs of visitors. The other one is in Boulder City, about 25 miles south of Las Vegas. Some of those zip lines have speeds of up to 65 miles an hour.

www.ingramcontent.com/pod-product-compliance
Lightning Source LLC
Chambersburg PA
CBHW061733020426
42331CB00006B/1234